How Not to Raise a Child

E. Maria Makepeace

ISBN 978-1-0980-3837-3 (paperback)
ISBN 978-1-0980-3838-0 (digital)

Christian Faith Publishing, Inc.
832 Park Avenue
Meadville, PA 16335
www.christianfaithpublishing.com

Printed in the United States of America

Preface

This year, Joan Parsons, our oldest parishioner, celebrated her hundredth birthday and died a few weeks later. For those who knew her, our clearest memory is probably the Joan of twenty years ago on Remembrance Sunday. As a churchwarden of eighty, she was still able to fit into her WW2 Wren uniform to lay a wreath at the memorials over there, and perhaps the action brought back memories of driving—without lights and at top speed—through docklands with bombs falling all around.

I was born after Joan's war. But if that war had not taken place, I would not be here this morning. If an English boy, not much older than Tom, our last year's choirmaster, had not killed someone of a similar age in the south of Italy, I would not be here today. That boy, who became my father, was alone behind enemy lines, taking photos of reservoirs, when he encountered a German boy, also on his own. My father, having survived the desert and Crete, had the quicker reflexes, the greater vigilance.

Later on in that war, up in the north of Italy, the Germans were retreating, burning all traces of their presence as they fled. A sheltered teenage girl, home on holiday from her convent school, saw what the Germans were doing. As someone hoping to study modern languages at Venice University, she foolishly approached the Germans to ask if they had books in German, which would be useful to her. Not long afterward, while the girl was with her mother in the garden at home, two partisans appeared, one armed with a gun and the other with shears. They sheared off her hair at gunpoint.

Later still, war ended; boy (my dad) meets girl (*la mia madre*) in Venice—and they marry. Without a need to prove her post-war allegiance, would this unlikely couple have married? They realized their mistake soon enough for themselves, though not soon enough for me. Wisdom in hindsight, perhaps—like the foolish bridesmaids in this morning's gospel, who forgot their flasks of oil and only realized their mistake too late.

To say that war brings out both the best and worst in people sounds like a platitude. Life may do that anyway; suffering may do that anyway. Our choices and lifestyles affect the lives, decisions, and behavior not only of ourselves but of those around us. They affect future generations too.

* * * * *

This is from the beginning of my sermon in St. Mark's English Church, Florence, Italy, on Remembrance Sunday of November 2017. I am the future generation of the English boy and the Italian girl, and Elner's story is my story—*How Not to Raise a Child*.

Chapter 1

Nelly Makepeace used to boast that both her sons came into the world on a bright, sunny, Whitsunday: Maurice on the twenty-sixth of May and Stan, eight years later, on the eighth of June. Decades later, a similar link never occurred to Stan when both his daughters, born twenty-one years apart, announced their forthcoming arrival during meals of fish and chips. From the sublime of one generation to the ridiculous of the next.

The first girl baby was born into postwar England during the worst years of rationing. The place that was to become her early home was a small two-story stone cottage with a wooden hut tacked onto the side of it and surrounded by a smallholding somewhere "in the middle of nowhere." No, perhaps slightly more geographical precision is called for. There is a place called Stanhope in Weardale in western County Durham in the Pennine Hills of northeast England. But the scene is not in the village; it is across the river and the railway, a place all on its own called Ward's Villa.

Remarkably for those days of limited transport, there is a car parked in the lane outside—Uncle Wilf's car. Wilf has an office job with the Coal Board and is married to "Aunty," who is Nelly's husband Fred's niece but brought up as his younger sister. Although Aunty's name is Evelyn, she is always referred to as "Aunty"—*the* Aunty.

It is a Friday night, and the family tradition on Friday nights is to eat fish and chips with Aunty and Wilf. The world outside is bleakly November with wind and rain; but indoors, the family had arranged themselves around the fireplace: Nelly and Fred;

Aunty and Wilf; Stan and that foreigner Fernanda, the wife he married in a place called Venice. Apparently, it has canals instead of roads!

Fernanda realizes that the baby is contemplating its arrival and alerts the others. She has just turned twenty-one, has only been in this strange country for two months, and is feeling very much alone among these alien *contadini*, as she sees them. The others, however, intend to finish their fish and chips before bundling her into Wilf's car for the journey to the "posh" maternity hospital twenty miles away in Bishop Auckland. They make it over Gasworks Bridge to the main road at Shittlehopeburn, but there they realize that they have to turn back, having bundled Fernanda into the car without her bag containing the nighties and baby things!

It is a bleak cold journey with the rain turning sleety. Sometime after midnight, the baby arrives. It is a girl. Better luck next time?

> Mere humans, born to finite lives,
> we yearn to set beginning straight—
> infinity grows "wild" beyond our walls.
> Mostly head-first, we whooosh into the world.
> The birth-light of creation dawns.
> Our baby fist begins to grasp
> before the eyesight can adjust to things.
> No, Dawkins: "re" creation.
> human life is more than genes.
> We're much more than some world-wise ants
> spread out beyond our means.

Fernanda sleeps, awaking after dawn to a bright snowy morning—misjudging it all as "beautiful." Her baby sleeps as well. Two lost girls to be visited later by the baby's father Stan, a lost boy of twenty-three. He was...

Her youthful misjudgement; her brief dalliance with romance,
As a student, aged 19, in Venice, just after the war.

Their wedding: St. George's Church,
Venice—(the English one)—then
her once-in-a-gondola's-lifetime/Cortina by snow.

Then: Stanhope's dire rationing. Weird-
Dale. Their small, squalling brat.

(She packed in that alien culture.
Alone, she went back).

Well, she did, but we're getting slightly ahead of ourselves.
We probably need to recap on this meeting of untrue minds. How
did this mismarriage come to pass? If an English boy had not killed
someone of a similar age in the south of Italy, I—the aforementioned
baby—would not be here today. That boy, who became my father,
was alone behind enemy lines, taking photos of reservoirs, when he
encountered a German boy, also on his own.

A lad of Weardale, sent out to scout,
lacks caution in exhaustion.

Another, of Bavaria, relaxed, unguardedly,
recalling native woodlands, views of home.

THEN! reflex answers reflex; face to face.
Survival speaks.
That bayonet's more silent than a gun

My father, having survived the desert and Crete, had the quicker
reflexes, the greater vigilance.

Sometime later, in the north of Italy, the Germans were retreating, burning all traces of their presence as they fled. A sheltered teenage girl, home on holiday from her convent school, saw what the
Germans were doing. As someone hoping to study modern languages
at Venice University, she foolishly approached the Germans to ask if
they had books in German, which could be useful to her. Not long

afterward, while the girl was with her mother in the garden at home, two partisans appeared, one armed with a gun and the other with shears. They sheared off her hair at gunpoint.

Later still, war ended; boy (Stan) meets girl (Fernanda) in Venice, and they marry. Without a need to prove her postwar allegiance, would this unlikely couple have married? They realized their mistake soon enough for themselves, though not soon enough for me. To say that war brings out both the best and worst in people sounds like a platitude. Life may do that anyway; suffering may do that anyway. Our choices and lifestyles affect the lives, decisions, and behavior not only of ourselves but of those around us. They affect future generations too.

Stan was Church of England, denominationally speaking, and Fernanda Roman Catholic. So, a month after her birth, the baby was christened in High Street Methodist Chapel because Fred had been the organist and choirmaster there for years and because the Westgate minister had an Italian Waldensian wife—the only other Italian lass in the dale. The baby's two Christian names, Eleanor Maria, represented her two grandmothers and her "stateless" state.

If Stan and Fernanda had lived in a home of their own, would things have worked out? Probably not. But living in with Stan's parents in rustic discomfort strained them to the end of their tether. Stan found work at Newton Aycliffe as a paint-works clerk but was later promoted to sales. He bought himself a motorbike and sometimes whisked Fernanda off to the pictures on it. That was a relief from her days spent with Nelly, Fred, and the baby, with the four of them imprisoned together.

Nelly disapproved of Fernanda's foreignness but tried to teach the girl the basic domestication previously omitted from her education. This, to Nelly's mind, prevented her from sweeping the dust under the carpet. Fernanda found the lack of basic facilities, stimulating conversation, and reading matter a constraint, though. There was no electricity. The family used paraffin lamps indoors and torches outside. The wireless worked with an accumulator. And although the Stephenson family's gasworks was only a couple of hundred yards away as the crow flew, the family had no gas oven either. Everything was cooked on the coal fire or in its oven.

Outdoors was the smallholding—the reason Fernanda thought of her in-laws as "peasants." Back in Italy, she had believed that Stan's address—Ward's Villa—was an actual Villa. Now she knew better, or did she? Fred was actually a retired quarry manager. As the seventh son of a lead miner, he had been allowed to go to Wolsingham Grammar School because his father and six older brothers could afford to let him.

Smallholdings, or at least a large allotment, had traditionally helped lead-mining families grow vegetables and raise a goat or cow or a few hens. Fred and Nelly expanded from this tradition. They had two cows; a pig; hens; turkeys and bees; Mickey the fox terrier; Tidgey the cat; Smooty, her kitten; a vegetable garden; fruit trees; and two fields. Once upon a time, there had also been a goat, who travelled by train on his own initiative to Frosterley and back. Nelly also crocheted, knitted, and baked and iced wedding cakes. Additional skills included ploating hens, lancing boils, and laying out the dead. She had left school the day she was thirteen and went into service at Cromer House, Frosterley.

As her new granddaughter grew, Nelly would tell her stories about the "olden days" as a schoolgirl.

"A tangerine at Christmas,
With a sixpence for a treat.
We'd get the strap if we were late,
from watching Blacksmith shoe great horses
on the road to school.

"...took Mondays off from Standard Seven's boring poetry.
Turned poss-tub's beat into the metre of a future life."

There was also an earlier memory. Nelly, aged three or four, along with her younger sister Mary, accompanied "Ma" to Frosterley Station. There, Ma's parents, younger brothers, and sister set off on a journey, first to the Yukon and later to Vancouver.

Their old world ends at Wolsingham,
is dying now along the Weardale line.
As Mary-Hannah and her toddlers shrink
into that old life's pitfalls—soil/ore/stone.
Beyond comes embarkation for a "whole half-world" away;
where trading lead for gold
and grief for more,
they'll still share thoughts and photographs
twixt their lass, Mary-Hannah, left behind,
and divers' folk to come.
They, westward,
mined in water sunset gold.

Nelly's father was a stonemason and steeplejack (including the steeple of Frosterley Church). For a time, her mother, Mary-Hannah, ran the bottom pub in Frosterley.

As Fernanda's baby learned to speak, Nelly became "Nonna" and Fred "Gagga." Stan and Fernanda became "Mammy" and "Daddy." Fernanda became an auxiliary nurse at Bishop Auckland, with long, hard, tiring shifts—often night shifts. She would return to Ward's Villa exhausted and irritable. Once, Fred was boiling some milk on the fire. Something he said angered her. She seized a sharp-edged dessertspoon and scraped it down his face, drawing blood.

She was so alone! There was no one on Fernanda's side, it seemed, as Stan was often "away" on his motorbike. And when he wasn't, he weakly sided with his mother. Rivalry ensued between Fernanda and the child's grandparents. As the baby began to crawl and then toddle, it became an exasperating, needy, and willful creature (in Fernanda's eyes, needing discipline by being shut in cupboards until any crying ceased), yet it was still glad to see Fernanda on her early morning return from work.

And so it happened. There was no gate on the upstairs part of the staircase. The toddler, who had been sleeping upstairs with Nonna, heard her mother downstairs talking to Fred, who got up early every morning to milk the cows and eat his breakfast slice of fruitcake! The toddler went to the stairhead, saw her mother at the stairfoot, and fell from top to bottom.

Pick her up, tell her to stop crying, and start toddling again. No doctor, no checkup, no X-rays. That was life back then for the future "clumsy" child. Any clumsiness, of course, was the child's fault. And why the heck did she have to walk splayfooted?

Another occasion. The Canadian relatives had sent Nelly some grey squirrel skins from Vancouver. Nelly set to work and made a grey "kitten" stuffed toy. The delighted child named it "Tidgey-Babbler" (translation: Tidgey's "bambina") and played happily with it. Then Fernanda returned from the hospital, decided the new toy was a health hazard, snatched it off the child, and took it to the kitchen sink—along with the kettle—slamming the door behind her. The child, shut out and so shockingly deprived of her new toy, wailed.

Nonna later returned the toy cat to the child when Fernanda was not around. "She's a bit dilapidated, mind." Fortunately, despite the odd bald patch, Tidgey-Babbler survived alongside the child for more years than Fernanda did. A while later, Fred and the child were crossing Gasworks Bridge, and the River Wear was in spate. The child observed the angry floodwaters and remarked to her grandfather, "By, she's dilapidated!"

As previously mentioned, Fred would rise early to bring in the "Jersey" and the "red" cow to milk. Nelly was not a morning person, but sometimes the child would enjoy going to the byre at milking time and (held in place by Fred) riding on the red cow's back as it was returned to graze in the bottom field. Mickey would pad along beside them too.

The byre brought security
of lowing cows, aware
of lower lights
and scents that mingled paraffin and hay:
both carried on a gentle draught
that made the lamp-light swing
its shadow-creatures on the whitewashed wall.
And all around, warm cow-coat smell,
and cow-muck, and a ruminating sound.
A comfort from their lifetimes' hopes,
they'd sown into their land,
with backaches, failures, disappointments and unnoticed ends.
No chance to turn back time—reverse such trends.

When the child was three or so, Nelly and Fred's older son Maurice decided to set up a guesthouse at Ireshopeburn but couldn't raise all the necessary funds. His parents decided that they were getting on in years, and maintaining the smallholding was becoming harder. They sold Ward's Villa by auction, and it later became Heather View Caravan Site.

"The largest caravan site in the dale,"
my once first-home is nothing like my childhood memory.
Its wheels and metal bodies pastel-paint infinity.
A toddler and her dog played roly-poly in their day,
when these "invaded" slopes were fields of hay.
But now? "Keep Dogs on Lead" and lead the way
to places tourists haven't taken in.

Nelly and Fred moved into what had been Maurice's house at St. John's Chapel. Maurice and his family moved to the guesthouse at Ireshopeburn and hired a school-leaver called Annie Wall to help them. Meanwhile, the little girl was about to discover village life and other children now.

Chapter 2

Stanhope was a large village, which claimed town status, having both a marketplace and market cross and a town hall containing a police station, courtroom, and large meeting hall (for dances, theatrical productions, the "pictures," and later, town quizzes). Several of Stanhope's buildings dated back to Norman times; a bridge was said to be part Roman, and there was even a more recent castle in ample grounds, although during the '50s and '60s, it housed an approved school. Stanhope vied with Wolsingham, five miles east, as the "capital" of the dale. Meanwhile, St. John's Chapel, eight miles west, or "up" the dale, was definitely a village, despite also having a town hall, a monthly mart, and a cobbled marketplace.

Back in the days when the move from Ward's Villa occurred, it was possible to work out exactly which settlement someone came from by their accent and use of dialect words. The further updale, the stronger the accent and the slower the Weardale drawl (veering toward East Cumbrian). Meanwhile, Rookhope folk, from the most northerly village, had a slight Geordieness to their speech. With the advent of television, Americanization, and southern "incomers" buying up cheap (for them) housing or second homes from the '70s onward, such local differences are no longer so pronounced. The strong sense of belonging has also declined from...

A friendly dale...with closeness in its limestone scenery.
Its villages well-interspersed with trees, shut-snug by fells.
The only clints or grikes in families,

14

whose surface hides divisions underneath that "Vedra" green.
Well-sharpened edges lurk in sunset grass

Living in St. John's Chapel, the three-year-old "Elner" (how the accent shaped her name) discovered that other children existed and had to be related to. Back at Ward's Villa, other children had never really featured in her existence. Cats, Mickey the fox terrier, and the two cows had all been friendly creatures. But Elner soon learned that human beings were a different matter and that she was not entirely welcome or accepted for several reasons, mainly thanks to her parents' activities, nationalities, and life choices but also because of her grandparent's Stanhope and Frosterley affiliations. The villages of the dale were both clannish and competitive. Thus, Nelly kept up her longtime allegiances with friends and family in Frosterley and Stanhope, while Fred still played the organ on Sundays at Stanhope High Street Methodist Chapel.

Elner remembered Nelly making "tea cake done in the oven" for Sunday tea before Fred went out to catch the bus down to Stanhope. Back in those days, when few people owned cars, the bus service was designed to fit the times of church services or vice versa, and this setup continued to the early seventies.

While Sunday was Fred's "night off," Nelly had two nights free: Friday (for Frosterley family, shops, and fish and chips) and Saturday for Stanhope friends and former neighbors. Generally, she would take Elner with her for safety's sake. Fred tended to lose himself in "Friday Night is Music Night" on the home service, and one Friday night, Elner had climbed onto the chair by the desk to open the "box with the hair in it" and had opened a pack of razor blades. Not knowing they were sharp, she squeezed them. Nelly returned in time to witness the beginnings of a "bloody mess!" So now, Elner was taken to both village outings, while Fred enjoyed his music night in peace.

On Fridays, Nelly would get off the downdale bus at Frosterley and proceed to the co-op store there, next door to the institute. First, she would stop in the downstairs grocery part, with high wooden counters and competing scents of ground coffee and cheese. Sometimes, Herbert Bainbridge, who worked there, would sit Elner on the counter, tell her he had a little girl of about the same age at home, and feed her a chunk of cheese. Elner loved cheese—and sardines, tomatoes, and *green vegetables!* Then Nelly would climb the stairs to the drapery and furnishings department to see what was new there. Leaving the store, they went down the street to Harry Burrip's paper shop, where Nelly paid for her "papers" (*Woman* and *Woman's Own* and sometimes a comic for Elner). The last shop was Fawcett's, where Nelly bought her weekly stash of Craven A and some Condor Slice for Fred.

When Nelly and Fred first moved to St. John's Chapel, Humphrey and Myra, with their children Billy and Myrtle, lived at the end of a terraced street behind Fawcett's shop. Humphrey was Nelly's youngest brother, a quarry owner and haulage contractor. A couple of years later, Humphrey's own detached house at the west end of Frosterley would be completed, and his family would move into something approaching luxury by postwar standards. Nelly approved of Myra, believing her to have good taste and judgment in all things.

Allowing Myra to see to her children's bedtime, Nelly would go on to her final Frosterley stop of the evening—Aunty's for fish and chips with fizzy pop. Elner was given a small glass, as befitted her size, and Uncle Wilf thought himself oh-so-clever, telling a three-year-old to keep her nose out of the glass when she drank! Then came the cold wait at the bus stop, with Elner snuggling under Nelly's coat to keep warm, while Nelly remarked that the moon was "on its back," so it was going to be a frosty night.

On Saturday, there was, for a year or two, a long torchlit walk to Parson Byres (the farm next door to Ward's Villa) to visit fellow neighbors Willy John and Joe Currah, Willy John's daughter Margaret, and Mag Harrison. They were well guarded from intruders (even those coming in peace) by a warlike gander called Jock. Elner was terrified of the avian guard!

Returning by bus on Saturdays was a further fear for Elner. Often, an elderly woman from Westgate would climb loudly aboard after a pub crawl and attempt to communicate raucously with other passengers. It was a great relief to the little girl when P. C. Gray escorted Mrs. McGurk off to the cells for the night for being drunk and disorderly.

When the journey was snowy one Saturday night, Nelly and Elner saw a fox galloping over a snowy field with a stolen hen. This memory remained years later.

> The snow is sliding by the byre wall.
> Nearby, a light hangs on the hill.
> It keeps star-height and still.
>
> A fox is moving in behind the dyke
> Half-hidden moves toward
> A scent that seems blood-warm.
>
> The farmer, on his settle, by the fire,
> Has locked the hen-house door,
> Assured of food to eat.
>
> The fox, already gone
> Leaves red prints with his feet.

When the family first moved to Roydene, St. John's Chapel, Fernanda was still around, still working at Bishop Auckland Hospital. On one occasion, a tall young blond Welshman called Bobby gave her a lift home, and he and Fernanda took Elner for a walk across the river, down the far bank where cattle were being pastured, and back to the village by the white bridge. Fernanda was nervous of some skittish bullocks, but "Bobby the Big Man," like a knight in shining armor, lifted Elner onto his shoulders to get them through the field quickly and safely.

Sometime later, Stan came home accompanied by a similar-looking tall young blond man. Elner immediately mistook him for "Bobby the Big Man," about whom Stan knew nothing. Oops! No; in fact, this was Ralph (pronounced "Rarrf" in Weardale), one of Stan's biker friends. Stan's wartime activities meant that he had missed out on his late teenage years, so now he was indulging in a regression to make up for those lost late-teenage years. He joined the updale gang of bikers—lads who were chased after excitedly by the local teenage girls, especially those who were skilled riders.

At one point, Stan won a large cup at cross-country "trials." That, along with his participation in the Fell Rescue when a plane came down, gave him the self-styled "black sheep" of the family, some sort of hero worship from the local lasses. Participation in amateur dramatic production *The Ghost Train* further enhanced his stardom. Annie Wall, a fifteen-year-old who worked for Maurice at the guesthouse, was smitten, as were her two younger sisters.

Older residents, however, viewed these bikers as a menace to law and order, as the "young hooligans" raced each other noisily from pub to pub or from fish-and-chip shop to dance floor, scaring locals with their speeding. Stan, being a not-so-young hooligan and a married man, ought to have known better than to be an early ton-up boy.

Fernanda's teacher parents, back in the Veneto, worried that their daughter was throwing her life away. If she insisted on being a nurse, then she ought to be a fully qualified nurse or even a medical student. She was bright enough. Soon after Maurice and Jessie's guesthouse became workable, they sent one of their ex-pupils, Giuseppe, to check up on her. Giuseppe stayed at the guesthouse and had long discussions with Fernanda in Italian, sometimes, sadly, interrupted by that annoying English child attempting to copy their speech and play the piano in the guests' sitting room, trying to tell the story of Little Red Riding Hood in sound effects. Soon after Giuseppe's departure, Fernanda moved to Newcastle RVI as a student nurse.

Student nurses, of course, were in contact with student doctors. One young anesthetist-in-training became particularly friendly with Fernanda, although, as he explained to Elner thirty odd years later, it was "all platonic, of course, back in those innocent times." But out of her uniform, dressed to the nines in her fashionable Italian clothes and flawless makeup, Fernanda became the personification of glamor on her return trips to Weardale and a source of envy for local village girls in the "back of beyond." On one occasion, when Fernanda came "home," her makeup was spread out on the dressing table. Little Elner was interested. When no one was around, she sneaked into the bedroom and tried to use it, the sort of thing most little girls attempt from time to time. But Fernanda caught her in the act and was furious.

Another "bad mammy moment" that Elner would later recall was connected with adapting to the new staircase at Roydene. It had a turning at the top. Elner felt that was dangerous, considering her past staircase experience at Ward's Villa, so she always kept to the widest part, descending seated. No doubt in some mistaken attempt to give her confidence, Fernanda sat herself on the widest steps and tried to persuade Elner to descend on the narrow side. No way!

> There's times of kindness.
> (Other times there's not).
> Dear parents, give my childhood your best shot.
> For childhood's short,
> and if it's short of you
> there's loss of heart, for what's a child to do?

Stan too would sometimes pounce; hit; send the child upstairs to bed; and then, repenting of harshness an hour or so later; would return to release her, bearing ice cream, distracting her from a game of cloud "pictures." The grandparents stayed aloof from such parental actions. By their "not interfering" neutrality, they proclaimed themselves to be not totally reliable.

While her parents were making their first moves toward stepping into their separate future lives, young Elner began discovering that others, adults included, were sometimes driven by self-centeredness, prejudice, racism, and jealousy in their dealings with her. At times, she was discovering a sense of aloneness that children with siblings rarely know. And before anyone translates "aloneness" into "mere" loneliness, the two conditions are very different. The first implies an irremediable solitary existence not of the person's choosing. The second merely implies a sense of sadness produced by a lack of like-minded others. Remember, this was not long after a war, which was still being fought every week in children's comics. Italians were depicted as the "comical, cowardly" enemy. Remember too that food was still rationed up until the day when Fred took Elner along with him to hand in the ration cards at the Ebenezer Chapel.

That road to bullying was yet to come in all its fullness later, when Elner started school, although there were already some uneasy hints of her "difference" being noted when she encountered some of the other older children. Preschool aged, though, Elner was often sent off for walks with Fred and Mickey-the-dog, while Nonna, the "boss of the family," had her afternoon nap on the chesterfield by the fire in the living room. Sadly, Fred objected to being seen with Betty, Elner's best friend rag doll, scruffy with use and with a handy hole in her bonnet so that she could be dragged along in pretense of walking alongside. "I'm not having that thing coming with us. Leave it at home." Walks were often long and involved technical explanations about lead mining (including not playing near shafts), quarrying, natural history, and local history (the village deep underneath Burnhope reservoir that once was alive).

At other times, Elner explored alone. Council houses were being built behind the greenhouse, where Fred had started growing tomatoes. The greenhouse was his refuge from Nelly, where he could smoke his pipe in peace. Soon after their move to St. John's, Elner had once been beyond the greenhouse with Fernanda, who was scavenging throwaway wood from the builders because it would come in handy as firewood. So, having learned how to climb over the low wall, Elner decided to scavenge by herself one day, only to discover that the house at the bottom of the garden now had tenants—a family called Wilkinson with two children: David, a top-juniors-aged boy, and Janet, a few months older than Elner. The Wilkinson children had a bouncy puppy too.

Nelly generally looked down upon people who lived in council houses. To her Victorian way of thinking, it was only one step away from the workhouse. However, the Wilkinsons didn't fit her class-ridden demographic theories. The Wilkinson husband's family owned a farm at the other end of the village, while his wife was well-spoken, an elocution teacher indeed. So Elner was allowed to play with Janet, who was deemed a "nice little girl." Nonna was not so keen on the other little girl from the council houses—Kathleen Wearmouth, who often played with Elner and Janet—mainly because Kathleen's father was a lorry driver, who worked for Uncle Humphrey, taking stone from his Harthope quarry to heavy industry on Teesside. Kathleen and Elner did not have a particularly calm friendship. Initially, it was very up and down.

For Nelly, foreigners were both frightening and inferior. There was that Jo-seppy for a start! If a French onion man or an Indian carpet salesman was on the loose in St. John's Chapel, she would skulk at the back of the house, never answering the door to them, hiding where she could not be seen from the window. And as for the postrationing Italian ice-cream men, she was suspicious of eating such "kelterment" in case the gentleman had stopped to relieve himself at the roadside while on his rounds and had omitted to wash his hands. She preferred a Walls ice cream sandwich from Mr. Elliott's shop. It came wrapped up in paper! Another of Nelly's fears had to do with technology. There was a phone box in the marketplace. One day, Nelly was required to use it. She dithered quite a lot before daringly entering this alien red box armed with pennies.

Elner's childhood tantrums were often blamed on her "nasty *Italian* temper," making her realize that she was "not quite one of them" (the one hundred percent English people within the family setup). Yet Nelly was her favorite adult, especially when she had a fall and was crying. Nelly would sit the child on her knee and sing songs from the "olden days."

"Daisy, Daisy"
"Wallflowers" growing tall.
Comfort from an earlier age
Before life's shadows fall.

Daisy, Daisy,
Grow inside this wall.
Take the comfort offered you
if nasty things befall.

Elner was often taken on visits to the guesthouse at Ireshopeburn. Uncle Maurice and Aunty Jessie had friendly cats, and the cats had kittens. Elner felt comfortable with cats more so than with fellow humans. In the grounds were various other attractions: Maurice's saddleback pigs, hens, Donald the Duck (a pet of big cousins Maxwell and Judith), a tennis court, fruit bushes, a secret garden with a bird bath, a grotto where Judith and her friend Evadne Chipper acted plays, a terrace where Aunty Jessie served teatime tomato sandwiches (sadly, well peppered), and a field at the very back where Maxwell and Judith had their bonfire and fireworks on the fifth of November. There were unpleasant surprises from time to time, though: dead hens hanging up by their feet in the kitchen porch, the butcher Oliver Humble turning up with his gun for pig killing. And, of course, the ghost.

Judith was eight years older than Elner and Maxwell six and a half years older. Egged on by Annie Wall, Judith and Maxwell decided to perpetrate a "joke." They told Elner to go into the cupboard under the stairs (in the dark, when being shut in cupboards was, to her, a Fernanda punishment). When she appeared reluctant, "Ah," she was told, there was going to be "a really exciting surprise!" It would be *fun!* So she waited for the arrival of the wonderful treat (?)…only to be confronted by a horrible wailing ghost coming toward her, blocking the door out of the cupboard. Annie Wall had given Maxwell one of the old sheets to turn into a ghost costume. Judith, the family actress, joined in the "sound effects."

But much worse things than this were about to happen. One afternoon, while Fernanda was still around, she and Elner were walking back from the guesthouse to Roydene when they saw a large plume of dark acrid smoke. Closer at hand, flames crackled, spat, and whooshed. The bungalow across the road was on fire. The (volunteer) fire brigade from Stanhope had been called but were eight miles away. Meanwhile, shouting, panicking villagers had formed a human chain, passing buckets from hand to hand. Fernanda joined in, sending Elner home to Nelly and Fred, who were watching the action from the front bedroom window. There were no survivors. The elderly couple who had lived there, along with their dogs kenneled outside, were burned to death. Exploring the embers a couple of days later, Fred pointed out to Elner where the dogs had died and remarking that both fire and water were good friends to humanity but bad enemies.

The transient nature of animal life was further emphasized when Mickey, by now an elderly dog used to roaming freely around Ward's Villa, had escaped from the front lawn only to be run over at the top end of the village. Elner wondered if there was a heaven for dogs somewhere. Human life was also transient. Nelly took Elner to a funeral at Frosterley, including the burial. This gave Elner nightmares of being trapped alive in a coffin!

Six weeks after Elner's fourth birthday came the horrible Christmas. Elner caught the measles fairly badly. She couldn't stand the light so was sleeping (when she could) on the chesterfield with a chair, covered in a sheet, shading her face from bright light. Even when the measles finally subsided, she was left with very painful bouts of earache. Meanwhile, upstairs, over that Christmas, Fred was suffering badly from pneumonia in one bedroom and Stan from gastric flu in another. Fernanda, being a student nurse, had to keep well away from these infections, so she spent that Christmas with a student-nurse friend and her mother in Sunderland. Nelly had to cope with her "emergency ward" mainly on her own, although with some help from Aunty.

A seasonal robin caused a superstitious scare by flying in through an open window and into Fred's bedroom. Despite that, no one died, and "Bobby Robin" was adopted and fed crumbs. There was snow in early January, and Dr. Thomson, calling in on his rounds, diagnosed a long winter by the way the snow persisted behind the walls up the hill.

Before another Spring
The roads will block with fresh in-blowing snow.
Then fields will almost fill
With floods, which turn ice-cold
Then melt away to spring.

And as the days go on
The river rushes, burn-fed, in its spate.

Floods last about as long
As local rumours stay
Before they melt away.

Before another spring
A lot of changes may be on their way.
But in this valley still
They deal in stones and wool,
Anticipate no change.

Janet Wilkinson, whose birthday was in July, started school after that Christmas. When everyone was well again, Fernanda, daughter of a headmaster and a teacher, tried to have Elner start school as well. After all, in Italy, the academic year followed the year of birth, and, even so, exceptions could be made for early starts. County Durham was a different matter, however. People like Janet, with a fifth birthday before September, could start school now, she was told, but those with birthdays later could not start until September.

That was the inflexible British law. She was to learn more unfavorable news of English law over the next couple of years.

Chapter 3

A nd so it begins:

In the County of Durham

Petty Sessional Division of Stanhope and Wolsingham (Stanhope sub-Division)

Before the Court of Summary Jurisdiction sitting at The Court House, Stanhope, in the County aforesaid

The 17th day of October 1952

STANLEY FREDERICK MAKEPEACE of Roydene, St. John's Chapel, in the said County of Durham (hereinafter called the Complainant) having made a complaint that he is the father of a certain infant named Eleanor Maria Makepeace

of which infant FERNANDA MARIA MAKEPEACE

of 25 Kensington Gardens Square, Bayswater, London W2

(hereinafter called the Defendant) is the mother and that the Complainant and the Defendant are now living separate and apart.

On hearing the said complaint and the facts therein alleged having been duly proved: and the court having regard to the welfare of the said infant hereby order that: the legal custody of the said infant be committed to (the Complainant).

The Defendant shall have access to the said infant on two calendar months of each year.

(Duly signed by the JP)

On the back (by purple typewriter ribbon):

Certificate of Service, Service of Process (Justices) Act, 1933 (illegible bit)

I hereby certify that I have served the defendant with the order, of which this is a true copy, by leaving it for the defendant on this day with another adult male person at her last place of abode.

(Duly dated and signed, but not by her mother, on 20th October)

And so, just a few weeks after Elner finally started school in September 1952, aged four, parental hostilities were out in the open.

"Inheritance"

The parents fed on sour grapes—with swift recovery—
though children's teeth are set on edge,
that's just how things must be.

Here's lifetimes drinking bitter wine and eating crumbling bread.
A penance for the sour grapes on which the parents fed?

(1980-ish)

It was Stan who took young Elner to school that first day. His preferred route to St. John's Chapel County School was the least visible one—down the back lane—although no one met them at the stile that particular morning. At the school gate, they were directed up the steps of the first building on the right, the prefabricated dining hall. Mr. Soulsby, the headmaster, sat just inside the door, meeting, greeting, ticking names off the list, dismissing parents, and directing new children inside.

Stan informed Elner she was not to cry, and off he sauntered. Cry? Well, of course she didn't! But what a strange classroom this was. The children sat on forms at the Formica dinner tables and gradually, as the morning passed, the place filled with a smell of institutionalized cooking.

The infants were in the dinner prefab for the first term. The winter was a cold one, and the place was heated by a coke-burning stove with a railing around it. Some days, the school milk was so cold that it froze in the bottles, and the children would hang their hands, holding bottles over the rail in order to melt their milk.

The Christmas party also took place in the dining hall. Mr. Soulsby called in and did a magic trick, finding a sixpence behind Elner's ear! He and his wife (and also Miss Craig later) lived near to Roydene, between the Roltons next door and Mrs. Peart, Nelly's crony at the petrol pumps. Nelly used to go to Mrs. Peart to get the wireless accumulator charged—and to charge herself up on the latest gossip. Those teachers who were near neighbors, Elner found to be more sympathetic, friendly, and helpful—more trustworthy, in her mind, than the others.

Apparently, right at the time when Elner was due to start school, the powers that be at County Hall, Durham, had sent painters there, and the painters had started work in the geograph-

27

ically farthest-flung infant classroom. There were four classes in all, educating children from four to fourteen: infants, lower junior, upper junior, and senior. It had, therefore, been decided that the infants would spend their first term in the dining room, while the other three classes were nomadically shunted about in the main building to avoid the painters.

The first infant teacher was called Miss Harrison. After a year, when her small charges surmised she had attained the age of a hundred, she retired. Miss Watson came in her place. Miss Craig taught the lower juniors, a younger man (was his surname Hill or Hedley?) taught upper juniors and art, while Mr. Soulsby was responsible for those who had failed their eleven plus and were hanging on for escape into the workforce on their fourteenth birthdays. Cousin Maxwell was currently in Mr. Soulsby's class. (Meanwhile, Cousin Judith attended the private Wolsingham Convent School, where they wore brown uniforms.)

To local schoolkids, that new Italian child Elner was recognized as "the enemy" personified. Youngsters in the early fifties read comics, after all, and many children's comics' popular heroes were still "fighting the war" or escaping from POW camps. Germans were depicted as tough, steely blond guys, but Italians as wimpy, comical brown "foreigners." Elner was "foreign" by association.

In addition, unlike the rest of them, she didn't have a "respectable" mother; that is to say, one who was tied to the home and slaving away in the kitchen. Instead, her equally foreign mother was off "in London being an air hostess," according to some local rumors! Meanwhile, her father was "a sort of pre-ton-up biker" with a sixteen-year-old girlfriend.

These parents were actually getting divorced, which was a scandal back then. Nobody except the aristocracy or the "guilty" got divorced in those days. (How times have changed! These days, probably half the students in any classroom have divorced or divorcing parents). So Elner, being the odd one out and through no fault of her own, was deemed fair game for bullies right from the start.

"Take that
Italian brat!"
"Hoy some chippens—make her scat"
"Sticks and stones may break my bones—
but only donkeys bray"
The schoolkid mob advances,
adults look the other way.
"And Fred, the grandad, Fred said:
"Interfering in children's squabbles is beneath our dignity."
"Children should fight their own battles.
It's not my place.
That's right! Save face.
"You have to fight your own battles now!" (And how!)

Fred and Nelly were not going to complain to the school. They made it clear to her, from their Victorian viewpoint, that "you have to fight your own battles." Taking this literally, she gradually discovered that her safest move was to aim a punch at the biggest bullying kid. Noses were a good place to punch, as a big kid's burst nose turned attention away from Elner and onto the bloodshed and tears of the assailant.

Unfortunately, this was unhelpful to Elner's reputation with some teachers. Thus, when Elner had been at the school for some months (perhaps a year), one home time, she was chased out of the school gate by a mob of all-age pupils with stones and pebbles. She hared off along the lane by Harthope Burn leading to the marketplace. There, she crossed the road and found the largest woman she could to hide behind. Next day, she went to school as usual, saying nothing to the teacher. (Where was the point?) Remarkably, though, her marketplace rescuer did have something to say. So, then, on that occasion, did the teachers.

However, although Elner was generally expected to fight her own battles single-handed, she was also expected to play a part in her father's divorce battle. Stan had acquired a newly qualified young solicitor to help him: Harold Hewitt, nephew of Charlie Pickering, their friendly travelling grocer. Harold was based in Bishop Auckland. He appeared at Roydene one evening to ask Elner some hypothetical questions about her future life and parents. Was it here, at the age of four, shortly after starting school, that she was taken to the courtroom in Stanhope and questioned? Or was it later, aged seven, when the real divorce proceedings took place? Or was it, indeed, both?

In her memory, there was some important reason for being upstairs at the town hall. The circumstances were upsetting, and she remembered later crying, weeping her heart out by the Rodham Monument at Newtown, waiting for the "updale" bus back home. It was years later, in her late teens or early twenties, when she was friendly with P. C. Gray's daughter Rina that he, the policeman on duty for such events, remarked that he'd thought it was a disgrace to put "a wee bairnie," smaller than his own little girl, on the witness stand.

(Let the reader understand, in this divorce case, Elner was confronted with her first "formal interviews," about which she would have a mental block in years to come. Unknowingly, it would affect her performance at job interviews, where, on occasions, sensing possible antipathy from questioners, her mind would become suddenly totally blank, even the question she was in the middle of answering vanishing from her mind.)

Look! Put me in reality—as, in that, I adapt.
Don't judge me like your win-case (brash or glib).
Your parfleche questions, drawn and shot,
then vanish from my mind.
How can I pin the dematerialised?

And do not ever—never ever!—
strive to make me cry.
You BULLY!
Why?

Once the first term was underway, school doctors arrived to check on the health of the new starters. They decided that Elner should wear a heavy patch over one eye (in pirate fashion) and that she needed an operation to remove tonsils and adenoids. During tatey-picking week, Nonna took Elner to the mart, where an obnoxious boy called Duncan, a year or so older, punched her in the eye patch. Thankfully, the injuries caused from this event saved her from having to wear the patch any longer.

Meanwhile Dr. Thomson, who, according to Nelly and Fred, had been an ENT specialist before his war service, reckoned that only the adenoids were a problem. "Oh, and how was the earache? Was it still bothering her? Was she wearing her bonnet in the winter winds to keep her ears warm? Be careful not to let her get colds too. (Her first illness as a baby had been whooping cough, which had left her with a weak chest.)

Stan borrowed Maurice's car and took Elner for an appointment with the "specialist" (consultant) at the RVI in Newcastle. She was to have an operation. In the fullness of time, an appointment would be sent.

This led to a puzzle. Where was Fernanda? Yes, at the time of the preliminary hearing in Stanhope town hall, her given address was in London. But was that temporary? Had she known what Stan was about to do and informed her parents? Perhaps their advice to her had been to find a "London" solicitor to represent her.

The point here is that when Elner was admitted into a children's ward at the RVI, she was looked after by a couple of Fernanda's fellow student pediatric nurses, who were still expecting her to return and continue the course. This put Elner slightly on edge. Would she see her mammy again while she was abandoned here in this strange place forty miles from home? She had arrived on a Sunday afternoon with Nonna and Aunty in Uncle Wilf's car. They unpacked her case, put her into the bed, and (wonder of wonders!) gave her a whole box of chocolates to enjoy. Sadly, the chocolates disappeared not long after the adults and were never seen again.

The ward filled up with other children—Geordie children with Geordie accents. They lived nearby, and their mothers, aunties, and siblings came in to visit them every visiting time. Elner's relatives, though, were several bus rides away. No one turned up for her again.

The operation happened in due course, with the Geordie children having their operations on the same day of this '50s Tonsil and Adenoid Conveyor Belt System. Elner was awake when she arrived at the operating theater. The anesthetist asked her if she could count to twenty. Well, of course she could…and woke up some hours later feeling woozy and vomiting.

The next day, all the children were recovering. All the others had parental visitors, sympathizing and bearing gifts (comics or sweets), as usual. Then, the following morning, the nurses told the children that they would be going home today. Little by little, the ward cleared—except for Elner. A nurse assured her that a telegram had been sent to her home, which had no phone back in those days.

Is anyone coming to claim me, as families do?
Or have they forgotten?

How long will they leave me like this?
The other kids trot off back home to a hug and a kiss.
I'm dumped—and nobody wants me, it seems.
No parent's apparent.
This kid wasn't part of their schemes.

At the end of the working day, Stan finally put in an appearance. "Ah, Mr. Makepeace, you received our telegram? You've come with the child's clothes, as requested, to take her home?"

Telegram? What telegram? He had come straight from work at Aycliffe on his motorbike. The telegram had been sent to his home address. No, he didn't have any clothes for Elner and could hardly take a convalescent five-year-old forty miles home as a pillion passenger in a nighty, now could he? Someone would have to collect her in the morning.

But the hospital staff needed the bed, so, tutting, they wrapped Elner in a tartan blanket, plonked her in a wheelchair, and loaded her in the back of an ambulance with several adult passengers, all of whom had to be unloaded at their respective (closer) destinations before Elner was finally delivered to Roydene by Ernie, the St. John's Chapel ambulance man.

On learning that she had not even had the opportunity to eat her chocolates, however, the feckless adults were sufficiently upset to provide her with a new box all to herself. When she was well enough to return to school, she learned that her rival Kathleen Wearmouth was now ahead of her in the reading book race. It was a lose-lose situation.

In medicals, ever after, she would be asked, "Do you have tonsils?" to which the logical answer was, "I don't know. I was unconscious during the operation. The trophy hunters may only have stolen my adenoids, but you're the medics, so why ask me?" She never used that logical reply, however. She just thought it.

Adults were exasperating, irrational, and untrustworthy creatures, some teachers (both infant and Sunday school) included. One day, after the infants were restored to their own classroom, Miss Harrison picked on Elner, especially, for something that wasn't solely her fault, but a general, inclusive group naughtiness in which she had been allowed to participate. She was the one hauled out of her desk, though, shaken round the class and then stood at the front, by the blackboard, as an example to others. Miss Harrison then stood at the blackboard, writing something on it. Elner, furious at the injustice, gave the frail sixty-year-old a push, which caught her off balance. Miss Harrison toppled gently backward, seating herself bottom first into the wastepaper basket!

Sunday school adults were equally unjust. Fifty yards east, on the other side of Hood Street, was the Methodist Chapel. On Sunday mornings, there was Sunday school, an opportunity for Elner's grandparents to have a peaceful morning. They believed that Stan should provide her with collection, so she had to shout up from outside the front door, hoping her daddy would wake up from his hangover open the window and toss down a threepenny bit or just a penny or two. Then off she would scurry in an attempt not to be late.

She started off in Betty's class. They met in the vestry. Betty worked "downstairs at the store" (grocery—upstairs was everything unperishable) and was a nice girl, but some of the other Sunday school adults and "big ones" weren't so nice. Before going off to classes, the whole Sunday school met together in the main chapel, being talked at, singing hymns, and saying prayers.

One Sunday morning, Elner was on the inside of the pew next to the wall, trapped, and the little boy sitting next to her was called David Crammond. He had recently had a birthday and had brought his new toy car with him. During the prayer, he drove it over Elner. She told him to stop it. He didn't. She thumped him. He cried. Result: the nasty little girl was put out onto the main street with the big door slammed behind her. The cheek of it: hitting the local preacher's son. No wonder she preferred sad music to cheery things. Her favorite hymn was "Jesus, Friend of Little Children," and her favorite popular tune was "With Broken Wings."

One day, for some reason or other, Stan was not at work, so he was home for dinner and told Elner he'd set her back to school afterward. At last! Some time with her daddy all to herself? Of course, they went by his favorite and more secretive route. There was a scent of honeysuckle along the small track round the council houses to the back lane. And there, sitting on the style, waiting for Stan to arrive, by appointment, was Annie Wall. She was no longer working for Maurice and Jessie at the guesthouse but with Rankin's Bakery by the bridge across Harthope Burn. If they walked together down the back road to the school, it would look like an accidental encounter, nothing more.

During her second year in the infants' class, Miss Harrison having retired, Elner's new teacher was Miss Watson. Teacher and child regarded each other with mutual dislike.

One morning, Mr. Soulsby came into Miss Watson's classroom accompanied by Stan. Elner was then asked (in front of a class full of small witnesses) if she was agreeable to having a day off school. If so, she could go and meet her mother for the day. She was so agreeable, if only to having the other children jealously watching her escape. Off she went with Stan to catch the downdale bus to Stanhope. There, the "hostage" was handed over to her mother for a day in Bishop Auckland. Both survived this encounter happily.

Some weeks later, in keeping with access agreements rather than educational demands, a longer visit to her mother was proposed. This time, Stan borrowed Maurice's car and handed Elner over to her mother at a respectable hotel, set in its own walled grounds at Witton-le-Wear. While Stan was still with her, Elner was promised the possibility of a new game called croquet. The hotel had a croquet lawn, apparently, so let's go and play before unpacking. Elner was duly taken off to play this "Alice in Wonderland" game. Stan left, with the chance of a car to play with.

Later, after the complicated game, Fernanda explained to Elner that the hotel was actually booked up for that night, so they would be staying up in the village tonight. They headed off uphill to explore. At the paper shop, Fernanda bought Elner a big paperback book about children from other lands and another, smaller one, on how to draw cartoons. They had fish and chips to eat and then went to an ordinary, comfortable room, where they would be staying that night—upstairs in the local pub.

There was a popular Italian song in vogue at the time, and Fernanda patiently taught Elner the Italian words. She read her the story of Meetik the Eskimo, and Elner slept, feeling secure. Next morning, they took their bags to the hotel and then went for a walk by the river, looking for Witton Castle. It was a fun day, despite a spot of rain, and things were still going well.

At Elner's bedtime, though, things changed. Fernanda was due to meet someone that evening in the hotel lounge bar, so from Fernanda's point of view, it was important that Elner went to bed and fell asleep as quickly as possible. From Elner's point of view, though, things were different. She was being left alone in an unknown, unexplored, featureless room in a strange place. All right. She was prepared to try that. She didn't want to be a baby. But at home, Nonna used to tuck her into a "nest," with pillows encircling her like a baby bird. She was allowed a light on and a book to look at or read.

"No!" There would be no light, no book, no nest. She would be obedient. This was a hotel. Fernanda switched off the light, shut the child in the pitch-black room, and disappeared to her important meeting in the hotel lounge.

If only Fernanda had played this differently. If only she had allowed Elner some light and a book. If only she had not cleared off to a licensed part of the premises, where no one under the age of eighteen was allowed.

In the hotel bedroom, the darkness became oppressive and frightening, empty and hostile. The child began to cry. She craved the safeness of familiarity. Her sobs grew louder and louder until Fernanda was requested to "do something."

In her own life, on this evening, Fernanda was also feeling frightened and alone in a strange place. This meeting with "whoever he was"—albeit for legal, work, or leisure motives—was important to her. In her nursing work, where she had to adapt to different shifts of duty and also needed to put her worries out of her mind, Fernanda had taken to using sleeping pills. So she went upstairs; gave the child a sleeping pill; put out the light again (oh, foolish young woman); and, leaving Elner alone again in the appalling blackness, returned to her important visitor.

Elner's adrenalin counteracted the efficacy of the tablet. She continued to cry, becoming more and more agitated. Panicking, Fernanda gave her more medication but, at her wits' end and perhaps on the advice of her visitor, also phoned Maurice at the guesthouse. Maurice drove to wherever Stan was (possibly the Wall home at Wearhead?), then had himself dropped off at Roydene, while Stan drove to Witton-le-Wear (accompanied by Annie Wall). Annie stayed in the car, keeping a low profile, while Stan went into the hotel, collected Elner, and took her home. For once in her life, she was plonked down on Annie Wall's knee. Perhaps the sleeping pills were, by now, making her drowsy. At least, she was on her way home.

This was the last time in her childhood that Elner was left in the care of her mother. Fernanda went to London to live, finding work as an international rep for Max Factor and Elizabeth Arden while awaiting the outcome of the divorce. Work took her back to Italy from time to time.

Chapter 4

"Red, white and blue.
The cat's got the flu.
The dog's got the chicken-pox
and so have you!"

That's what the schoolkids of St. John's Chapel were chanting in the run-up to the coronation in 1953—even the half-Italian child. While the little girls in the infants' class discussed what red, white, and blue clothing they were going to wear on the big day, Stan, in competitive mode, was secretly waxing artistic in Fred's shed with half tires, paint and brushes, soil and seedlings. He was going to win the village's Best Coronation Decorations competition. Meanwhile, Maurice had invested in one of those newfangled "television" things for the guesthouse so that the family could witness the great event on a tiny black-and-white screen. History was now, in North East England, in the world around and outside of Elner's problems.

She did have friends by now, despite still being regarded in some quarters as an extraterrestrial, the closest being Janet Wilkinson, Kathleen Wearmouth, and Barbara Scott. All three had "proper" families with parents and siblings. Elner always found this "family" aspect interesting as a sociological phenomenon. But whenever called upon to play "houses" among the big river stones littered at the bottom of the school playground near the burn, she would opt for playing the naughty child part. (In this "pretend game," there were limits to pretending for her. She was unsure of how the parental concept was played out in domestic reality.) She preferred playing schools or cowboys and Indians, where she chose to be an Indian. There were also skipping and ball games on offer in the playground, but she wasn't much good at either.

With Janet, one of their favorite games was pretending their toy stuffed dogs were real and taking them for walks. The two little girls swapped comics. Elner was allowed Robin (and later also, as her reading improved, the *Enid Blyton* magazine). These she exchanged for Janet's big brother David's *Eagle*. On the front cover of the *Eagle* was Dan Dare, Pilot of the Future, introducing the interesting topic of space travel. There were also episodes of Dan Dare's exploits on Radio Luxembourg, which Elner was allowed to listen to while plowing through her suppertime porridge (breakfast was generally a mashed banana with "the top of the milk" on it).

Janet's collection of children's books was different and interesting too. Elner particularly liked the illustrations in Janet's *Pookie*—the trees and colors depicted there. She had decided likes and dislikes in both illustrations and colors. Further "culture" presented itself when Mrs. Wilkinson learned that someone in Stanhope had started a children's dancing class. She and Nelly would take Janet and Elner to this class by bus once a week. The teacher had lived in Poland before the war, and her classes were held on the top floor of Stanhope Store. Most of the other children attending were "Stanhopers," so Nelly knew some of their parents and was able to introduce Madge Wilkinson to them.

After a while, it was decided that ballet lessons should also be held in the institute at St. John's Chapel, where Janet and Elner were founder ballet members, so to speak. But then, yet another rejection occurred in Elner's uncoordinated young life. Mrs. Polish-name decided to have a ballet performance in St. John's Chapel town hall. Janet was to take part, but Elner was too clumsy and asked to leave the class. Sad but wanting to watch how the others fared, Elner attended, along with little Jennifer Davis, from the middle pub in the marketplace. Along with all the dance items, there was also a string puppet show,

Afterward, while the dancers were changing or being congratulated by their proud families, Elner and Jennifer were allowed on the stage to see the puppets at close quarters. Elner worked out how to move them, while Jennifer, being small, wriggled into the puppet theater. Elner moved the puppet she was working across to greet Jennifer, and—*flash!*—the *Auckland Chronicle* photographer shot the scene, or at least the scene within the puppet theater!

On the following Thursday, all the dancers, Jennifer, and the puppet were featured in the *Auckland Chronicle* and in the black-and-white photos adorning Mr. Bee, the newsagent's window. Double disappointment!

Not that Fred approved of any of this publicity nonsense. There had been the occasion when Elner took part in the *Auckland Chronicle*'s children's coloring competition and won. Fred took her and her postal order to the post office, of course, to deposit the *whole* half crown in her Post Office Savings account (which Elner, however, regarded as her future horse fund). "And you're not to tell them where you got this money, mind," Fred warned her, as if winning a coloring competition open to all South West Durham were a blot on the family escutcheon rather than some vague achievement!

Friendship with Kathleen Wearmouth was less artsy or cultural, more competitive (the race through their reading books) and intellectual, at times more name-calling and warlike. Interestingly, it was generally when Nelly and Mrs. Wearmouth clashed over some childish squabble between the two little girls, so that they were banned from playing with each other, that Kathleen and Elner were most friendly. The subterfuge and the adventure of disobedience made them allies. They would meet up out of sight and trot along to school together, discussing the possibility of life on Mars or the fact that if, as Sunday school assumed, everyone sprang from Adam and Eve, they must be hundred-and-something cousins. Therefore, their disobedience was entirely justified. They also compared swear words used by their fathers. When allowed to associate, they would sometimes attend the "pictures" together in the town hall, usually Westerns, and they would stand for the national anthem at the end, as was the custom back then.

Nelly was still mobile at this time, so Elner could look back on at least one happy neighborhood picnic excursion on foot, along with Mrs. Wilkinson, Janet, David and his friend Guy from a cottage near the railway, Mrs. Wearmouth, Kathleen, Sheila, and their baby sister Susan. This group walked up Chapel Fell, veering east, then south, passing a frog-spawn pond, and eventually heading down the Slit Burn valley to the place with the waterfall. There, the youngsters plodged in the burn, David and Guy courageously explored the cave behind the waterfall, and the whole group sat around, eating their picnic food, totally undisturbed by any tourists (this was still Weardale's pretourism era). Then, tired out by the exertions of the day, they caught the bus back from Westgate to Mark's Well.

Elner's friendship with Barbara Scott was about freedom from the Victorian rules of home, about adventure and a love of the countryside, about feeling accepted. Barbara was the third of four children, and for a time in the infants' class, she shared a desk with Elner. When she started school, her eldest sister, Jean, was already at the grammar school, her brother Peter was in top juniors but was soon to pass his eleven-plus and follow Jean there. Her little sister Sheila was over a year younger.

Unlike Janet and Kathleen, whose gardens were adjacent to Roydene so that Nelly could keep a stern eye on play, Barbara's parents lived at a place called Four Lane Ends, up a cart track beyond East Blackdene. There was a proper "back road," which ran past their house. It linked Daddry Shield to Ireshopeburn (and West Blackdene) without passing through St. John's. But at Four Lane Ends, it intersected with the East Blackdene cart track/road to the fell top. The Scotts had a smallholding downslope from their house and a small triangle of mainly evergreen woodland in the angle between the East Blackdene lane and the back road going to Ireshopeburn.

Nelly would send Elner off to the Scotts to play all by herself. Usually, she went by the black pipes bridge and the East Blackdene route. The most frightening thing that happened to her on these journeys was passing a farm where a cart horse was having its tail docked. Sometimes, on her way home, she picked flowers, whose names she knew, for Nonna. At other times, being late and liable to get wrong, she ran until she got a stitch from running.

The Scotts were without either running water or electricity in those days. It was generally Peter's job to shove a barrel on wheels along the back road behind Scotts Wood to a tap, where it was possible to fill the barrel with fresh spring water from the fell. A little farther along that road, around a bend and well downslope, there was a small council tip (well, area for dumping unwanted goods). This was a real treasure trove for children building camps in Scotts Wood, who were looking for building materials, furniture, old pots, pans, and kettles. Less enjoyable was the fact that the "sanitary facilities" comprised an indoor tin bath in front of the fire and an outdoor earth closet in an outhouse! (But the proximity of the wood and the homemade roundabout more than made up for that!)

There was a glade in the wood with a little stream running through it. Harebells grew there. They called it Fairy Glen.

Through milkmaid fields to woodland harebell time.
Becoming clearer, there's Scotts Wood; Scots pine.
This clearing has a baby burn that tinkles through the trees.
This Fairy Glen's a place to please
a child torn by conflicting loyalties.
This place is clear and sharp. A scent of pine.
Beyond this spot life's trees are hard to climb.
Those children who have knees all scraped
and sore may never soar...

Then, come the rain, we'd scurry off indoors.
In pre-electric gloom we'd sit and draw
around the oil-clothed table, as the well-known lines took form
into the outline of a borrowed home.
Years on from Elner's past, Scotts Wood's regained.
Scotts' bairns all, now, successful, and about their own careers.
And yet, their parents had, to hand,
that drawing from their past, in detail, by a six-year-old.
That little, lonely child who came to play.
These memories in no way turn back time, although they stay.
Perspective makes things easier to say.

It was the stability, evenness, fairness of Mr. and Mrs. Scott that quietly helped Elner at this time. They never used corporal punishment or raised their voices to their children. It was their acceptance of Elner that was so helpful to her just when she needed such help.

Oh, Nonna was Nonna, of course. She was Elner's rock and headed the list of family adults to be loved in Elner's life. She was the boss of the Makepeace household, keeping Fred and Stan in order. She fed, comforted, and gave love to her grandchild, sometimes seeing Elner as the daughter she'd never had. And yet, there was an unevenness to the relationship, at times a discipline/ownership verging on cruelty, although she would never have understood this. This granddaughter, with looks too Italian too—much like Fernanda, her departed foreign mother—was a burden Nelly would have to bear into her old age until her death. Feel guilty, child; feel guilty for it all.

And that sense of drowning? It was Barbara Scott who saved Elner, literally, that time that long gone summer. On one of the few hot days of the year, after school, Barbara was going plodging upstream from the white bridge. Elner was allowed to go with her because initially, Peter and Jean were around with a big fully inflated inner tube of a tractor tire. They could swim, anyway. But after a while, they had to go home to do their homework, leaving Barbara and Elner in the care of some "big girls," who preferred to sit on the bank beyond the river stones, sunbathing and gossiping.

Elner and Barbara were plodging in a smooth but slippery mossy area, which, however, had a sudden dip into a three-foot deep faster-flowing gully leading to a miniwaterfall. Barbara had a pair of old hand-me-down sandshoes to plodge in. These gave her a good grip, and she could walk on the stony bits without hurting her feet. Elner was not so well equipped. She had to plodge barefoot, slipped on the slimy rock surface, and tumbled back down into the gully. She struggled to grasp the edge to find her footing, to not swallow water! Panic! Then calm. Why fight it?

Meanwhile Barbara Scott, perched on a rock above the gully, was shouting to Elner to grab her hand. Elner was loathe to continue the struggle, though. It would come to nothing; she would fall back again, swallowing yet more of the foul treacle-brown river water.

Barbara insisted. Elner raised a hand, and she grasped it and pulled. Elner's feet lowered to the gully bottom. She stood, and Barbara helped her out, got her to the towels and clothes by the big girls.

At that point, the big girls took control, sending Barbara to Roydene, while they wrapped Elner in a towel, thumped her on the back, encouraged her to sick up river water. Once content that a dramatic death was not about to happen, they returned to their chatter, waiting hopefully for Superhero Stan to arrive and carry home his drowned rat bairn. Instead of which—oh the disappointment—here came Fred with the out-of-breath Barbara, the overworked heroine who had quietly and sensibly saved Elner's life and then run for help. Thank you, Barbara Scott!

After a time, while Elner and Barbara were still in the infants' class, Mr. Scott took on a part-time job as school caretaker. Elner's teacher that year, following Miss Harrison's retirement, was Miss Watson. She was extremely "no nonsense." Education was not about enjoyment, for goodness sake, and heaven help any child who stepped out of line!

On one occasion, for no particular reason, she confiscated Elner's hat and put it in her desk. Elner was not allowed it back at home time. When she arrived at Roydene, her welcome was, "Where's your hat?"

"Miss Watson took it off me."

"Right! I don't want you having earache again. Get yourself off back down to that school and get your hat."

By the time Elner returned to the school, all teachers had left the building. It was now Mr. Scott's realm. "Hello! What are you doing here?"

"Nonna sent me back to get my hat."

"Where is it? Have you lost it?"

"No. It's in Miss Watson's desk."

"All right. If you know where it is, go and get it then."

(It was always more worrying to be in trouble with Nelly than with Miss Watson.)

On another occasion, Miss Watson put Elner in the porch for some imputed misdeed. Elner knew that repatriation in the classroom would involve corporal punishment and decided that, as dinnertime and punishment seemed equally only about ten minutes away, the solution to the problem was to set off for home at once. She walked to the marketplace and hid round the side of the public toilets until the midday updale bus stopped in the marketplace. It was then safe to walk slowly home and have her dinner.

Strangely, nothing of a punishment nature happened on her return to school! Miss Watson would have had to report the disappearance to Mr. Soulsby, who was kindly disposed toward the child, who lived two doors away, and to her parental problems. He must have told Miss Watson to calm down, suspecting with some amusement that Elner would have possessed the good sense to go home and eat!

After the second year in the infants' class, Janet and Barbara were to go into Miss Craig's class. As they had birthdays in July (Janet) and August (Barbara), they were technically, just to say, junior age already. But there were one or two more spaces in Miss Craig's class, so which of the infants should be promoted early?

"Kathleen Wearmouth." (Miss Watson's pet was an inch or two taller than Elner, so she looked older.) Then a couple of the boys were suggested…

Elner, not wanting to be stuck here without her friends, raised her hand. Miss Watson ignored this. "Yes?" asked the headmaster.

"Please, sir, I'm two months older than Kathleen Wearmouth, and we're both on the same page of the reading book."

"Right. You as well then. Come and join the others at the front."

(Ah, the sweet taste of freedom from tyranny.)

In Miss Craig's class, learning became enjoyable and proceeded at an interesting pace. They progressed to cursive writing, first in pencil and then using ink. Elner was awarded stars for her compositions. Some notion of English grammar was taught, and during her two years (no, one and a half, but we'll come to that) in this class, "sums" required all the "times tables" from two to twelve. During her final term, which would have been bottom juniors in a larger school, she was doing long multiplication and division and knew her fourteen and sixteen times tables because "stones, pounds, and ounces" sums required bases fourteen and sixteen.

There was a class library, and Elner took home *Robinson Crusoe* and read it herself. In class, they were reading *Black Beauty* in the original as their English literature project. Much more interesting than the tedious repetition of infants' reading books! They did "music" with band instruments: triangles, tambourines, and James McCorkie (usually) on the only drum. Education became interesting and fun. Elner felt that Miss Craig actually liked her instead of regarding her as a displaced nuisance.

She decided she wanted to be a teacher when she grew up—definitely not a nurse (the only other career option open to girls in those days)—mainly because Fernanda had been a nurse. She lined up her dolls and teddies along the chesterfield and chalked their lessons on a new blackboard and an old-fashioned folding slate. However, it then occurred to Elner that the bottom of the staircase was a better classroom site. She arranged her class on the bottom three stairs and was well into her game when Nelly descended from bed changing with an armful of washing, tripped on "those bally dolls," and sprained her ankle. Back to the chesterfield and to the doghouse!

As Elner progressed to a more mature stage, so did her father. Stan was approaching thirty. Even his younger biker friends were pairing off and considering settling down: Ralph and Ruby, Donnie and Molly, Neville and Eleanor. Clifford and Ann. Stan marked his new maturity by selling the Norton and buying a secondhand van. He had side windows and a back seat fitted to it. Then he painted it himself—bright green. It was to be known as "Edged" because it was EGD 810.

And with the arrival of Edged, interesting new adventures happened. First came a very cold winter. Windows at Roydene were covered in frost patterns in the morning. Farms up beyond Lanehead were cut off by deep snow for long enough to have used up their livestock fodder. The excitement of planes dropping supplies was happening! Elner was packed into the van in her wellies and just one pair of socks.

At Wearhead, Stan picked up Annie Wall, and off they went, through Cowshill, and up beyond Lanehead for this winter spectacular. However, the adventure involved standing around in snow as well as walking to a vantage point through snow higher than a child's wellies. So snow had already slithered down the inside of the boots even before all the cold standing around. After they had seen the full spectacle, they returned to Wearhead for tea at Mrs. Wall's. Mrs. Wall was a widow. Her husband had been a lead miner in one of the few lead mines still working in the dale. But Mr. Wall had died a couple of years earlier of silicosis.

Elner was frozen, her feet especially. Sitting by a fire with her cold wet socks off, she was in pain as the circulation gradually returned. Annie's younger sisters Jean and Lilian thought that was hilarious. Having lost their father, they regarded Stan partly as a father figure and resented the appearance of his daughter. Stan never understood any of this, though. He was just pleased to be admired and looked up to by females. One of Fernanda's mistakes was to be obviously better educated than he was. With Annie Wall, he felt surer of himself,

A more interesting adventure took Elner to an "almost foreign" land. Nelly's Canadian cousins (Ivy, Vi, and Myrtle) had visited her during the late '20s or early '30s, along with a friend called Betty Blair, whose mother lived at 33 Balbardie Avenue, Bathgate. Nelly had been in Christmas cake contact with Mrs. Blair ever since the Canadian relatives visited. Every Christmas, her production line of Christmas cakes was also parceled up and posted off to the Canadian cousins to Mrs. Roberts at Whitstable and to a Mrs. Chalmers in Yorkshire. During December, Elner got to scrape out a lot of cake dishes after the mixture had been put in the oven. Christmas pudding making was even more fun, though, and she was allowed to help with that.

Now that Stan had a van, Nelly persuaded him to take Fred, Elner, and herself on a day trip to Scotland! First of all, they visited the Forth Bridge (the railway bridge, that is) before heading on to Bathgate. Of course, in those pretelephone days, no one had thought to contact Mrs. Blair except by letter, and if someone is not at home, they obviously don't receive the information. When they knocked on Mrs. Blair's door, they realized she wasn't at home!

Ah, but just a minute. Neighbors appeared helpfully, providing the address where Mrs. Blair was staying with other family members in Glasgow. So they all piled back into the smoke-filled Edged and headed Glasgow-ward as the hunt for Mrs. Blair went on!

Finally, they found her in a flat in a Glasgow tenement block with other family members, including children. Elner was sent off to play with them. Remarkably, she found herself immediately accepted in a way that would not have been possible in St. John's Chapel. She and the other wild children hared around, playing hide-and-seek in bombed tenement ruins nearby. It was great fun. Then they all had tea, and Elner's family piled back into Edged and headed over the hills to their home in Weardale.

One of the big events of the year for the Methodist Sunday school kids was the anniversary. In the weeks beforehand, as well as learning their piece, the little girls taking part would be taken off (by parents in everyone else's case) to a "big city" like Bishop Auckland or even Darlington to find an anniversary frock, new ankle socks, and summer shoes. This would then be "Sunday best clothes" for the rest of the summer. At this time, angora wool boleros were all the fashion. One year, Nelly knitted Elner a white bolero; the next year, a pink one. As she strolled toward the chapel in her new attire, she saw her headmaster, who described her as a "Fuzzy-Wuzzy pink angora bunny."

When she was more normally dressed and encountering him out of school, however, his more usual greeting to the seven-year-old was, "Spell pneumonia for me." He knew she could do so; Miss Craig had told him. Elner had needed the word for a sad composition about Johnny the kitten, recently deceased. Johnny, a grey and white descendant of Jessie and Maurice's cat tribe had come to her in the following manner. Stupid Stan remarked that he had a surprise for her and plonked the surprise on her shoulders, where she couldn't see it. Something prickled her, so she shook it off. A poor little kitten fell to the floor. Elner felt guilty. She had hurt the poor thing! But she hadn't known it was a kitten or she wouldn't have hurt it. Adults were so stupid. Why hadn't they handed her the kitten gently? Poor Johnny had a short life, dying of pneumonia while still in his infancy.

Nelly's Friday and Saturday evening jaunts continued. One December, upstairs in Frosterley Store, Elner found a book with lovely illustrations and beautiful words: *A Child's Book of Hymns and Psalms*. She was so taken with it that Aunty bought it as her Christmas present. There were some variations to both Fridays and Saturdays as a result of house moves, however. Myra and Humphrey, Billy and Myrtle had now moved to their wonderful new house. Nelly was full of admiration for it. Hadn't her littlest brother done well for himself? Meanwhile, Joe and Mag were now living in Albert Terrace—actually, in Stanhope. Parson Byers had been sold and Joe and Willie-John had retired. Willie-John had invested in the newsagent's shop on Stanhope Front Street for Margaret to run. She provided Mag with copies of *Woman & Home*, which had a children's page with weekly adventures of the cut-out dolls Nora and Tilly. This kept Elner out of mischief while the adults sat in the living room, nattering, while the black-and-white photos of prize sheep judged by Joe and Willie-John looked down benignly on them

But one Saturday evening, Elner couldn't concentrate on Nora and Tilly. Her back itched. She sneaked out of the room and sat on the bottom stair, where the grown-ups wouldn't tell her off for scratching her back. Eventually, they discovered her there in her misery and checked up on what was causing the irritation. Chicken pox!

The lighter nights had arrived. Outside, behind the greenhouse, two new council houses were being built, and all the other children were playing chasey round the scaffolding. The town hall pictures were showing *Doctor in the House*. Kathleen and Janet were going. She'd heard it was good, but Elner was stranded in bed, itchily grumpy, missing all the fun. She was not amused when Dr. Thomson's newest assistant came to visit the patient and pointed out that she had a real doctor in the house, not just a doctor either. There was a new grey and white kitten to make up for the chicken pox and the loss of Johnny, but what could she call this new female kit?

"When I was a boy," the new doctor said, "we had a cat called Blossom." Blossom it was, then, and Blossom, unlike her late relative Johnny, did not get pneumonia.

By the fifth of May in 1955, Elner was back to school. Miss Craig took her class out for a walk over the now-trainless railway (a victim of the Beeching Axe) over the river (by way of the white bridge) and across the field to where the hill slope started, and there were steps cut into the footpath. Miss Craig sat the children on the steps. The sun was shining, and the birds were singing.

"Today is a very special day," announced Miss Craig. "It only happens once every hundred years. Today, the date is 5/5/55."

School was fun; learning was enjoyable; there were friends sitting around her and a teacher who liked her. Her world was expanding. Her daddy had a van! Elner felt she belonged.

Chapter 5

> The giant of the fairytale
> Is lurking all the while
> Beyond the books and play.
>
> Most children feel it should be right
> That giants are dispersed
> Through slings or magic rhymes.
>
> But here the giant still remains
> And will not be dissolved
> In floods of magic rains.

While Elner was enjoying her new stability regarding friendships and school—drawings, books, and play—while she was doing her complex "sums" and getting them right, her grown-ups were working on their sums and finding what would become the wrong answers.

Stan and Fernanda's divorce was finally "achieved." They were both making new starts in their respective countries. How had things been left between them, though? They had been married in a time of martial law in Italy by a military chaplain at the English St. George's Church, Venice. (But forty years later, Fernanda said that they had had to remarry in England at the time the divorce was finalized in order to be "officially" divorced in England. To some extent, a part of her was still "hypnotically" in love with Stan in spite of the hurt and anger at the forefront of her emotions.)

The court ruling was that the "child" was to remain with her father. Elner would not see her mother again until she was sixteen. She would not even hear from her again until she was ten or eleven, although Maurice and Jessie stayed in touch with Fernanda, who, hoping for a change of fortune, was now calling herself "Francesca," her third name.

Stan had now left his job as a salesman for the paint works. Instead, he was involved in "something" up on the fell between Stanhope and Middleton-in-Teesdale. And maybe the person he was working with was noted as a bit of a wide boy" cutting a few corners, and possibly needing an influx of cash? Meanwhile, Stan was now a free man. His divorce was past and gone, but it still had to be paid for, as had his dates with his girlfriend Annie, now working as a cook at Stanhope Castle Approved School.

Meanwhile, Maurice and Jessie were finding that the guesthouse project was not working out as well as they had planned. Maurice had continued his office day job for Redmires at Wolsingham. But increasingly, he felt like the little boy with his arm in the hole in the dike, holding back the flood. He was gradually becoming ill with worry. So while Elner began her second year in the stability of Miss Craig's class, adult machinations were afoot to disrupt her life once again.

Nelly and Fred needed to give away their savings to help out their sons. The plan was that Maurice would sell both the guesthouse and Roydene, then he and his family would move into a terraced cottage along the road from where they were currently living. But in order to sell Roydene, Nelly, Fred, Stan, and Elner would have to move elsewhere. Nelly and Fred had always missed their Stanhope and Frosterley friends, so a move eight miles downriver seemed to be a good solution for them. But where could they go that would not be costly financially? Buying was not an option, nor was renting. Fred was well into his seventies by now, and Nelly approaching seventy. The solution opted for was financially not costly at all, but it would become increasingly physically costly for Nelly as the years went by.

Fred, Maurice, and Stan were all Freemasons in the Stanhope Lodge. Fred was its organist—and a provincial grand organist to boot.

Thus, when Mrs. Hayton (a woman around Nelly's age or slightly younger), who had been the cook/caretaker of Stanhope Lodge but was finding the work onerous and wanted to retire to live with family in Hunwick, the menfolk suggested that Nelly could take over. There was a tied cottage across the yard / car park from the lodge. Nelly, Fred, Stan, Elner, and Blossom the Cat (successor / younger sister to Johnny) could move in there, it was decided. Nelly—aided by an aunt's backup team of Jessie, Evelyn (aka "Aunty"), and Myra—could help Nellie with the cooking once a month on Wednesdays. Oh, what a good idea!

Some weeks after the new term started for Elner at St. John's Chapel County School, this move to Stanhope happened. At that point, happily, there was no talk of moving schools. Elner was old enough to catch the updale bus from Stanhope Market Place to St. John's. At this hour of the morning, the bus was fairly empty as most people would be travelling to work downdale in Stanhope, Wolsingham, Crook, or Bishop Auckland.

As the bus travelled up the dale, fellow pupils would board it: a big boy called Campbell Jackson, and then at Camber Keels beyond the "aerial flight," Helen and Alan Drysdale, the grandchildren of Elner's former neighbors the Roltons, who now lived across the river in the hamlet of Brotherlee. Alan Drysdale was in Elner's class. Helen was a couple of years older and good at arithmetic, so from Camber Keels onward, the journey was spent discussing and explaining Elner and Alan's homework and testing them on their tables.

On the return journey, there was often a bus conductress who showed Elner how to make boats and airplanes from bus tickets. Fred and Nelly disapproved of this bus conductress, so Elner decided she was a friend, regardless. Another maths-and-bus-ticket phenomenon back then involved the children's adding up the numbers on the ticket in the hope they came to twenty-one. A "twenty-oner" was lucky!

The new home was along the Front Street in the east end of Stanhope and was called Greenbank. The main road from Daddry onward downdale to Wolsingham ran along the northern side of the river terrace above the Wear. The "back" (south-facing) windows of this new home had metal frames, which rattled whenever there was blasting up at Newlandside Quarry. There were only two bedrooms. Problem: Nelly and Fred didn't sleep together. Nelly explained this as Fred's liking a lot of bedclothes while she didn't. So normally at Roydene, Elner had to sleep with Nelly, while Fred and Stan had rooms of their own.

Now, Stan was given the smaller but warmer room above the living room and next door to the airing cupboard, while the rest of the family slept in the bigger long cold, damp bedroom with its sloping wall above the cold, damp rarely used sitting room. While the bathroom was at the top of the stairs, it had no lavatory, only a bath, washbasin, and the airing cupboard. The loo was located downstairs, beyond the living room and kitchen, by the back door.

Nelly decided that she and Elner should sleep in the big bed, while Fred had the single bed at the sunny side of the room. He liked a lot of warm bedclothes while Nelly didn't, Elner was told. Elner was given no choice in the matter, although she knew that children more often shared with siblings than with adults. Some even had a room of their own, the lucky things! However, and of course, directly after the move, Elner had to pretend because of the aunts helping with removals that she was the occupant of the little bed, so Aunty (or Aunty Jessie or Myra) made her say her prayers there. She was told to pray especially for Uncle Maurice. He had just been taken off to hospital with duodenal ulcers and was very ill.

Elner didn't really like her new home, although it was good to have a big yard / car park with the possibility of roller skating on the smooth part near the living room window. A few years later, having inherited cousin Myrtle's tennis racquet, she would play solo tennis against the wall of the next-door house, where the Hobsons lived. There was often a coke heap outside the lodge's coke house in the winter snows that could be turned into a sledge chute. There was a split-level garden too, which had grown wild. The upper level outside the lodge dining room windows had a large holly tree, which came in useful that first Stanhope Christmas. Nelly could hang out her washing at that level of garden, though she first had to lug it across the car park and down the side of the lodge along a narrow passage.

There were some pretty, scenic steps down from the washing-line level leading to the sloping lower level, where there were several fruit trees to climb or make hideouts around. At the bottom of the garden was a small gate leading out to Tinkler's fields. Fred and Elner would give the Tinklers a hand with their haymaking for the next few years. Later, those fields between the garden and the station would be turned into the Bondisle Way housing estate.

But Elner did not like the lodge itself. The kitchen smelled of gas. The whole downstairs interior was dark and spooky. There was an unpleasant feel to it. It was not the sort of place where one wanted to be alone. Possibly, her feelings were totally irrational, but she did not like the lodge at all.

Sometime after the move, possibly during the tatie-picking week (half term), Elner was not at school. So when a knock came to the front door, she was sent to answer it as the adults both had "bones in their legs" (the usual adult excuse for not doing what they had no wish to do). When Elner opened the door, she was confronted by two official-looking men in suits and ties, who proceeded to interrogate her about her father's employment. She answered the questions to the best of her ability and knowledge, being a clever little not-quite-eight-year-old. And she was later in big trouble for doing so. She should not have answered any questions, apparently! She should have called Fred or Nelly straight away. Why hadn't she? Well, the men were asking *her*, and the adults had bones in their legs. *Sigh!* She could never do anything right.

Soon afterward, for some reason, Stan changed jobs. He went to work in the Redmires office at Wolsingham along with his older brother Maurice, no longer convalescent...

Now, of the three aunts in her "cabinet" or "coven," Nelly's favorite was Aunty Myra. Nelly regarded her as the most ladylike. Myra's husband, Humphrey, Nelly's youngest brother, was only two or three years older than Maurice, and in childhood and their teens, the two lads had been more like brothers. Nelly had frequently helped look after her younger brother, so Humphrey and Maurice grew up as close friends. Then, with the start of the Second World War, Humphrey, in a reserved occupation, was not called up, while Maurice volunteered for the RAF. He became a pilot, was sent to Southeast Asia, and played double bass in a jazz group called the Java Jivers.

Stan, on the other hand, was eight years younger than his brother. When Stan was still a small boy, Fred began to suffer very badly from sciatica and overdid his input of aspirin. This would soon have its effect on his system. But Stan was a rumbustious little imp who tried Fred's pained patience, so Aunty stepped in.

Aunty (Mrs. Evelyn Phillipson) was actually Fred's illegitimate niece but brought up more like a younger sister to him. She was raised a staunch Methodist, all her life attending Bridge End Chapel at Frosterley. Aunty had married Wilf, who worked at an office job for the NCB. Wilf had been gassed in the First World War. Aunty and Wilf were unable to have children, so they took Stan under their wing whenever Fred's sciatica bothered him. They probably spoiled him. Aunty always saw Stan as a "son substitute."

But Aunty had never really approved of Stan's marriage or Italian wife. Conscience sometimes makes people overreact in the wrong way. Although Aunty was kind in some ways toward Elner, bringing her chocolate every Friday, she was overly judgmental in other ways, making Elner feel (as the rest of the family often did too) that she was never quite good enough, that in some way or another she was flawed, not quite a proper member of their family.

Recently, a family with an Italian mother and Irish father had moved into the institute over the road from Aunty, who lived at the Battlement. Aunty, who acted as Aunty to the whole village, took this "poor" family under her wing and showered them with kindness, frequently pointing out to Elner what a paragon of virtue Renata—this family's half Italian child—was.

Aunty Jessie was more influenced by and loyal to her own mother, who did not meet with Nelly's approval because she had been allotted a greater grandmothering role, in the lives of Judith and Maxwell. Because of Nelly's prejudices, though, Jessie and Maurice had regarded Fernanda as a victim during the last seven or eight years. They still kept in touch with her when no one else did.

This three-aunt committee then was Nelly's think tank and the recruits to her lodge cooking team. Of the three, the one favored most by Nellie was the dainty Myra, who positively sparkled with cleanliness. This liking proved unfortunate for Elner. At that time, Billy, Myra's elder child, attended the posh private Durham School, while Myrtle, the dainty younger blond child, attended Wolsingham County School, where she was in the "scholarship" year. Myra boasted to Nelly about what a good school it was and how much Myrtle enjoyed going there. Now that Stan was at Redmires, wouldn't it make more sense to send Elner to school at Wolsingham as well? Stan could take her to school, and she could catch the bus back, with Myrtle to look after her. This school was three miles closer than St. John's Chapel, after all, and it had such a good reputation…

So Elner was informed that in the new year, she would be going to a new bigger and better school. She said goodbye to her St. John's Chapel friends. She had already missed them at Sunday school, for no sooner had her "family" made the move to Stanhope than she had been sent off to High Street Sunday school on a Sunday afternoon at 2:00 p.m. This meant that Mrs. Collins, the minister's wife, who taught in the Sunday school, would arrive shortly after 1:30, doing a round trip of Dales Street, Union Lane, East Lane, and Martin and Graham Streets, collecting all the Sunday school recruits of all ages—various Dougalls, Greens, Carol Graham, and others. Such a silly time of collection meant that she often had to eat Sunday lunch alone as Nellie and Fred would not eat until Stan returned from his Sunday morning pint (or several) at his pub of choice, the Grey Bull. If Annie had finished her lunch time shift at the Castle, Stan would hang about and pick her up whenever she got off work.

So Elner, dressed in her best, had to eat alone, wearing a stupid pinny in case she spilled anything on her best frock. Elner loathed that pinny! She would sit there in solitary state, glumly munching to the sound of *Two-Way Family Favourites* on the home service.

Back at St. John's Chapel Sunday school, in early September, they had entered Elner for the seven- to nine-year-old girls' solo singing at the Circuit Youth Eisteddfod on the last weekend in October. She had been looking forward to it and seeing her friends on a Saturday. But using the move as an excuse, Fred vetoed that. He was never happy about any singing or choral activity she undertook, despite her enjoyment of singing. In addition, his second organist "Aunty Maggie" Irwin's husband, Ernie, was the High Street Sunday school superintendent. So, no, Elner would not be allowed to participate in the Eisteddfod, singing "I'm a Little Squirrel." End of story!

Christmas arrived, and the break from St. John's was even more final. Elner lay in her chilly bed, listening for Stan, doing his Santa Claus activity downstairs. Nelly came to bed, moved Elner over to the cold side, and snuggled herself into the prewarmed side nearest the lamp to read her women's magazines and suck her Black Bullets. However, the new Christmas morning brought a welcome surprise—a bike! Admittedly, it was Myrtle's old bike, which Myrtle, going on for eleven, was deemed to have grown out of despite the fact that she was daintily only a couple of inches taller than Elner. It was a midblue color, and in her dreams, Elner would have preferred red, but blue would do. It was a bike; that was the main thing. It was more than she had ever hoped for—the best Christmas present ever, even if she had disproved the existence of Santa Claus in the process!

There was a cold, frosty spell after Christmas. By order of Nelly, the bike had to be kept in the lodge dining room. Fine, as long as Fred went into the lodge with her and helped her learn to ride between the rows of tables. When Elner was proficient enough, they took the bike south (on the pavement) to the back lane, crossed the river, passed the gasworks, and Elner could ride from their old home of Ward's Villa to a disused railway crossing beyond Railway Terrace.

Nelly thought that Elner could now put the bike away by herself. Elner objected; she was not going into that spooky place alone. Why couldn't she keep it in the sitting room? No one ever used the sitting room except at Christmas and New Year. A compromise was finally reached; the bike would be kept in the lodge kitchen.

With the New Year over, Elner was taken to her new school and enrolled therein. She was placed in the class appropriate to her age-group. It was dreadful. They still printed instead of doing "real writing." They wrote in pencil, not in pen and ink. Their sums were tens and units, progressing to hundreds, tens, and units. The other children all lived at Wolsingham or on farms round about there; the outdoor toilets stank; and the playground was featureless, ugly, and all tarred over. And there was the business of having to cope with bullies all over again and even one or two teachers for whom the war was more real than memory.

She had to stay for school dinners in a huge echoey central hall, where children were served according to age-groups and made to eat everything. After a few days, she was feeling too sick to eat anything at all, so she was sent home early, only to find Aunty Mame (Nelly's sister from Stanhope Hall) and young Antony (motherless half cousin, Aunty Mame's grandson, who lived with her) tucking into Nonna-cooked food. Antony, apparently, went to Stanhope Barrington School and had the day off for Epiphany. If not St. John's Chapel, there were two perfectly good schools in Stanhope where Elner could have met and befriended local children. But, no, for Nelly, Aunty Myra was the expert at such things.

So there we were. Life was totally changed in a space of four months. Elner now lived in a spooky place with no friends. Far from being an enjoyable challenge and a place of security amid other life changes, school was now dull and insipid. Elner was forced in on herself in that new cold house. She read and wrote, drew and painted; her solace when all else was failing her was her imaginary world and the chance to lose herself in a book.

Chapter 6

There came a day—not a school day—when Nelly called a "summit conference" of the aunts. Fred took himself off for a walk up the street. Elner was left downstairs to her private play (or so they thought), while the aunts and Nelly took themselves off along the passage to the far bedroom, shutting the door behind them.

Obviously, this was something that Elner was not supposed to know about. So knowing by now which floorboards squeaked in the upstairs passage, she cautiously sneaked upstairs and crouched near the bedroom door, listening intently.

There was indeed exciting news! Incredible news! Elner had a little brother out in Italy, but that in itself was not the exact cause of the meeting. Apparently, Fernanda was claiming something called "maintenance" from Stan. This was some sort of payment for the new baby's keep. "What," Nelly asked the aunts, "are we to do about all this?"

Elner did not hang about to hear the rest of this conversation into alleged parenthood. Stan and Fernanda had apparently produced her. Now, her mother wanted money from her father for this new baby boy. Why all the secrecy? She crept back downstairs before anyone suspected that she had listened in. When the adults returned to the living room, she was seemingly deep in some Elner drawing and writing activity, seated in the small chair by the wireless and to the right of the fireplace. The seat where, Nelly often grumbled, she sat "like a hothouse plant" instead of "playing in the fresh air." (It never occurred to Nelly to wonder where Elner was supposed to find a playmate when she lacked the opportunity to meet other Stanhope children.)

Some days later, Nelly decided to inform Elner that Fernanda had had a baby. It was a boy, Nelly told her, and Fernanda had always wanted a boy as boys were more important to "them" (Italians). If Elner had been a boy, she would have been called "Michael," so this baby boy had been given the Italian version of the name she would have had had she not turned out to be just a disappointing girl. Now that Fernanda finally had a boy, she certainly wouldn't be wanting Elner anymore. Elner was, safely, all Nelly's property now. Nelly, after two sons, had always wanted a daughter. But Elner couldn't help wondering if a granddaughter who was bonny, blythe, and good; blond; and always neat and tidy and with "hockey legs" would have been closer to Nelly's ideal.

However, Elner churned over the baby boy and maintenance information in her mind, perhaps just out of curiosity for the where-abouts of this sibling—perhaps also from a wish to see what Italy was like. One light evening, when Stan had gone off on a date with Annie, Nelly had popped down to Mag and Joe's, and Fred was listening to music on the wireless, Elner made her move. She sneaked upstairs and hid under the bed in Stan's room. From there, she could open the lower cupboard section of the utility chest of drawers, in which Stan kept his private papers, including magazines of topless blond women lying around on sandy beaches. But all that she could find otherwise pertained to the divorce or Stan's time in the army. There was nothing about that mysterious baby boy.

The tedium of school continued. She was in Mrs. Morgan's class, and Mrs. Morgan's favorite girl and boy were Valerie Stirling and David Brown. Another bright boy, Stewart Skilbeck, had a lovely singing voice and had won a place at the Durham Chorister School. He would go there in the autumn.

Valerie Stirling was always given the best female role in any play. She was good at games too and always top of the class because she was expected to be and because she was a Wolsingham product. Besides, to Elner's mind, this school was boring! Arithmetic, reading, and writing offered no challenge and no expectancy that her efforts would be appreciated. Disinterest and lack of stimulation led her into carelessness. Elner was fourth out of twenty-five at the end of that academic year. Numbers 1, 2, and 3 were Valerie, David, and Stewart, as ever. Her boring school report read only, "Shows satisfactory progress. A neat, steady worker." This was something of an anticlimax after her last St. John's Chapel Report:

> Has a natural love for reading. Enjoys and appreciates books. Recitation very good. In composition sentences are well constructed and ideas good. Writing careful and painstaking. Arithmetic capable and reliable. Art very good. History and Geography very good. Illustrations in these subjects are outstanding. An intelligent pupil who is showing outstanding ability in all subjects.

Why, oh why, did Nelly move her?

At Wolsingham, there was also a greater emphasis on games and PE. Elner's clumsiness didn't help her there at all. She was always one of the last to be chosen for sides and regarded time spent on rounders or practicing for sports day as being akin to purgatory. Her growing pains didn't help. She just didn't fit in with the new regime.

One afternoon, Mrs. Morgan had to go away early, and some of her class were handed over to one of the male senior teachers who was stern and had been in the army during the war. He picked on Elner for no reason and made her stand up for the whole lesson with all the "big kids" looking on.

On the other hand, though, some of the senior girls (the top-class fourteen-year-olds who acted as playtime prefects) stood up for her to their fellows. Elner knew which of them was on her side because a few of these girls hung about in the morning to swoon over Stan, their apparent heartthrob, and wave timidly at him as he dropped off Elner for school. Elner found their attentions embarrassing, irrational…but also useful in times of playground strife. She also looked on the formula of "shake hands and say you're sorry" totally hypocritical. "Look, I'm sorry for being picked on because I'm different and don't belong. I don't want to be here, but I am. Whenever someone hits me, I don't start crying and come here to tell tales. I hit them back. And the next time someone attempts to bully me, I'll probably burst their nose too."

Despite Myra's promises to Nelly, Elner saw little of Myrtle, except on the bus home, although she remembered fondly one summer day when they were allowed to spend the long dinnertime playtime in the school field. With one or two classmates, Elner was going through the end-of-term play on the outdoor stage. Valerie Stirling went home for dinner and wasn't yet back, but Elner knew the main part off by heart. Myrtle, along with a couple of other eleven-year-olds, was watching and enjoying the performance until Valerie Stirling showed up, marched up to Elner, and ordered her off the stage because she—the star—was back now to do "her" part. Myrtle, however, stepped in and told Valerie to let Elner continue with it for now. Valerie, after all, would have her starring role in the "proper" performance, just as she always did.

This was the only instance that remained in Elner's memory of Myrtle at Wolsingham County School. At the end of those seven months of Myra's marvelous vision of their being together at the same school, Myrtle left. Having failed her eleven-plus, she was to attend a private school, The Mount, at Bishop Auckland. Meanwhile, Elner was stuck in that school for another three years.

In art, however, Elner excelled, and Valerie Stirling did not. She also enjoyed the BBC Schools' programs *Time and Tune* and *Rhythm and Melody*. Out of school, Sunday school also became more interesting when "scripture exam" studies started. Nelly and Fred allowed her to take the annual scripture exam, although drawing the line at other competitive out-of-school activities, such as music or singing. Perhaps a further reason was that the scripture exam was free? Elner was awarded honors and given a certificate with a pretty picture and a host of signatures. Mrs. Collins, her Sunday school teacher, was pleased. Fred and Nelly took it in their stride.

At home, meanwhile, Elner learned how to climb the wall taller than her, which divided "their" yard / car park from Hobsons' garden next door. The Hobsons, Billy and Cilla, had two children. Kay was a couple of years older than Elner, and Billy junior was a couple of years younger. Sometimes, if Stan was around on a Saturday, the Hobsons would climb over to Elner's side of the wall, and they would play backyard cricket, with a butter pat instead of a real cricket bat.

It was through Kay that Elner first learned about the Stanhope Lending Library. Kay took her along while returning books, so Elner joined too, enjoying the wonderful children's selection of both fiction and nonfiction. In time, Fred also joined the library, usually selecting cowboy books. He enjoyed cowboy films too at Stanhope pictures and sometimes wished they would make cowboy films in Weardale, with its wild, fell scenery and disused quarries.

Sometimes he would take Elner to the pictures with him, so that Nelly could have a "bit of peace" to knit or sew. They would sit somewhere in the middle seats of "upstairs at the town hall" because the Castle Boys from the approved school used to sit (segregated from the Stanhopers) in the front few rows. When the film snapped and darkness fell, the Castle Boys would stamp their feet until either someone flashed a torch at them or the picture returned. In later years, this activity was accompanied by a few voices chanting, "Torchy, Torchy, the battery boy!"

Among films Elner liked was one about a very small Scots boy called Geordie, who eventually, after years of teasing, had a late growth spurt and became an incredibly tall and strong caber thrower at the Highland games before being scouted for the Olympic team, either to wrestle, box, or throw smaller objects to win medals.

Another Scotland-based film was *Brigadoon*. Fred even took her to Wolsingham pictures once on the bus to see *The Inn of the Sixth Happiness*. The "greater love hath no man than this" scene had her in tears. But there was one film that really terrified Elner. It was about someone who went to the Himalayas, captured a yeti, and took it back to London. There, the yeti escaped and hid in the sewers, making forays out to kill people when it felt hungry. This gave Elner nightmares. Most films just featured cowboys and Indians, however. They were Fred's favorites.

Another nightmare was brought on by a combination of Sunday school and learning about the washer boys in the lead mines of Weardale less than a century before. In the nightmare, she was in the main room of the county school, used on Sundays by the Sunday school as the High Street Methodist Chapel was next door. During the first, corporate, part of Sunday school, after the introductory hymn, Uncle Ernie would pray at length, but Elner would peep and squint, taking in her surroundings. Behind Uncle Ernie, there were low cupboard doors set into the walls. In Elner's nightmare, however, naughty children from Mrs. Morgan's class (herself among them) were shoved through these doors into a cavernous place of fire and darkness to drag heavy carts full of stones forever.

As Stan persevered with his new job at Redmires, he bought a new van in place of Edged. It was a rusty red color and, with the registration number TPT 763, was named "Teapot." The new van had side windows and a back seat with a space behind, presumably for luggage. But with four adults to accommodate in comfort whenever Stan's girlfriend, Annie, was free, Elner tended to be given a cushion and deposited there for longer journeys.

Elner realized that it was possible to hide there as well because Stan usually left the vehicle open. One evening, during the school holidays, she learned that Stan and Annie were going to see a good new picture at Consett, something that she would enjoy! So she stowed away—off they went—without noticing her. Sadly, she misjudged her timings and made her appearance too soon after they had driven up Crawleyside Bank and over the cattle grid. Thus, she was returned to Nelly in disgrace and sent to bed early, while Stan and Annie went off to enjoy themselves.

Of course, it was not just Nelly and Fred who rode around in Teapot. There was an RAF base somewhere on the fell tops to the north of Stanhope, and Annie's younger sisters had now arrived at the lad-chasing age. The RAF held dances some Saturday nights, and Jean and Lilian wanted to go. Annie volunteered Stan to take them there, and it was there that both girls met their future husbands, Ron and Martin.

But somewhere up on those fells one Saturday dance night, a taxi driver was found murdered, so detectives came prowling around Stanhope, interviewing people, including Stan. Somewhere in her mind, Elner wondered if they would decide he was the murderer and arrest him. He did have quite a temper at times! She remembered being allowed to have Barbara and Sheila Scott from St. John's to play with her at Stanhope one Saturday. They were sitting around, eating dinner (lunch), laughing and joking, as children did elsewhere, when Stan took exception to Elner's enjoying herself, grabbed her from her chair by the scruff of her clothing, dragged her off to the lodge kitchen and pummeled her. She didn't even know what she had done wrong. The Scott girls were really shocked as their parents never used corporal punishment on any of their four children.

Elner still loved her daddy, though (usually), although he spent more time with Annie and her sisters and brother than with Elner. The Wall kids had claimed him as a father substitute, as well as "big sister's boyfriend." However, Nelly did not approve of this liaison, nor did she approve of Annie's claims as a cook. Annie was to be kept out of *her* kitchen on lodge nights—Elner too. Elner, with school the next day, had to go to bed at the proper time, so who better to babysit than Annie?

This arrangement suited neither put-upon party. At the start of the new school year, as the fairs started moving into Stanhope for show weekend, Elner learned of the peashooter (pluffer) battles between top enders (west of the marketplace) and bottom enders (from the east). Instead of shooting peas (wasteful in those times in North East England), green elderberries were used as ammunition. Elner wanted to join in to meet other children, so she slipped the leash and did not return at the correct time. Maybe the church clock wasn't working, or maybe Elner hadn't bothered consulting it, but Annie Wall, in full war paint, stilettos, and frills, came out to collect her.

"Oh, look," one of the top enders a couple of years older than Elner mocked. "There's your mother come to seek you!" To have such disgrace heaped upon her as having someone believe "that" Annie was her mother was unbearable. (Her mother was in another country, with a new baby who had replaced her—a boy baby, more loveable than she was.) Elner turned her fists on the older girl, totally ignoring her father's girlfriend. She was, after all, no relation and no symbol of authority. She was just "a big girl" all clarted up! Regrettably, Annie's love for Stan caused her to wallow in and drag Elner off toward home among taunts from the top enders.

Often at these babysitting evenings, they played a game of "piggies." Elner was the little pig, and Annie was the wolf. Sometimes, this included the wolf administering Chinese burns to the little pig.

The lodge had put a phone in the house, so Nelly had had to come to terms with it gradually. Sometimes, one or other of the blooming lodge men would wander in to use the phone. It made it seem as if the place was not home as Roydene or Ward's Villa had been, what with that big girl giving her Chinese burns and bossing her around and stray men using the phone on the stairs.

At times, the phone was useful, though, and Elner had a retentive memory even for numbers she had not actively learned. One day, Fred was in the lodge by himself, possibly practicing on the organ or the piano. Suddenly, he needed to get to the toilet, where he collapsed.

Nelly went to seek him to tell him dinner was ready and discovered him. Stan was at home, so it must have been a Saturday. Nelly and Stan flapped to and fro, panicking, while Elner went to the windowsill on the stairs, found the telephone directory, and looked up a number. Then she shouted at the panicking adults, "Phone the doctor. Stanhope 297." (Five or six years later, at school camp at Beadnell, Elner would wake from a nightmare in which she was shouting those same words. She had not remembered the number consciously and had to check it on her return from camp. It *was* the doctor's number!)

The adults got themselves to the phone; the doctor rushed along the hundred yards or so to the lodge. Fred had duodenal ulcers, which had hemorrhaged, but the doctor had arrived in time. The adults had been afraid that he may have been dying, and their fear tinged Elner's childhood too. Nothing was ever forever. Fred and Nelly were old.

That gave her yet another strange dream. She was running up to the top of a hill, trying to escape. Her pursuers wanted to inject her with something that would give her immortality, yet she was very afraid of them and struggling to escape. She woke, wondering why immortality should scare her so much. Outside, the amber of the street lamp shone from the darkness into the little side window.

The village yawns to night again
With branches tossed in frenzy
Above the churchyard gate.
Their suddenness of action
Is morbid contradiction.

The oldfolk wheeze and fetch the coal
(The coalhouse nearly empty
Because the cold came early).
They go and rake the grate.
They rarely wait up late.

The village stretches into night—
From cities into worlds.
From old folk knotting up the hews
To light tomorrow's fire,
To those whose death's the latest news—
Whose village does not sleep.

Chapter 7

Myrtle was not the only one who moved on. Stan would be moving on soon too. Soon, Elner would have both parents in different countries, although Stan's "other" country would be Wales.

In September '56 Elner moved from Mrs. Morgan's class to Mr. Davison's. He was a young new teacher and Elner gained a slight trust that he was fairer toward her than Mrs. Morgan had been. He was a Wolsingham lad, whose family farmed some land uphill behind the school field and the headmaster's house. So instead of the usual nature walk along Waskerley Beck, the class explored the fields and hedgerows of the Davison Farm. And at the end of that year, her report said: "*Well done*, Eleanor. A good term's work. Her work is always neat and of a high standard." (There was an "excellent" for English Language too.)

During the winter of that year, however, Elner had her usual bad cold. But Nelly was always reluctant to keep her off school, so she was packed off as usual to endure five miles of standing up, choking on the extremely smoky bus. (So where was Stan on that day? Was he going off to work earlier or later? Or did taking Elner to school only happen for the two terms of "bottom juniors?" Perhaps he had switched to going to work with Maurice and Maxwell by then, using their car?) Back in those days, there was assembly every morning, and one school morning, Elner had a bout of coughing that drowned out the headmaster. Afterward, he asked her if she was taking medicine for her cough. "No, sir, no medicine," she replied truthfully. So she was sent home with a note to the effect that "this child" was "not taking anything" for her cold, had to be "taken to the doctor" and remain "at home" until the cold departed.

Nelly, unable to be angry with Mr. Golightly for giving her orders regarding her treatment of the child, took it out on Elner instead for this letter. "You told that headmaster I wasn't giving you anything for your cough, but I've been making beef tea specially!"

Poor Elner was treated as a liar, although the headmaster had specifically asked about medicine, which she was *not* being given. Fred was made to take Elner to the doctors. She coughed in the waiting room, and it sounded like whooping cough (again—she'd had it as a baby). The doctor appeared to see who was coughing, jumped her up the queue (in the interests of not having a whooping cough epidemic on his hands), handed out a prescription, and told Fred that Elner had to be kept warm.

How did Nelly deal with this ultimatum? She left Elner to freeze in bed in that cold, damp bedroom until around 4:00 p.m. Well, all right. She was allowed a hot water bottle, but the air was cold. Only after Nelly had taken her usual afternoon nap would she allow Elner to come downstairs and occupy the chesterfield that Nelly no longer needed—wrapped in Nelly's dressing gown and a blanket. The warmth was a great relief when it finally happened.

Elner enjoyed the toasted homemade bread slathered with butter and the cups of tea brought up to her on a tray during her illness. If she had a spell of coughing through the night, Fred would go downstairs and bring butter and sugar balls for her to suck.

During her waking hours in the cold, damp bedroom, Elner read to amuse herself. She tended to read whatever came to hand: Nelly's women's magazines the *Beano* and *Dandy*, articles previously skipped in children's Christmas annuals, shop stock from years ago that "Aunty Margaret" Currah at the paper shop was getting rid of, and the more interesting articles in the set of encyclopedias (usually stories from the classics or articles about other countries). But during this particular illness, her favorite book was an old specimen copy of *The March of History to the End of the Middle Ages* by E. H. Dance, MA, published in 1930. It contained interesting social history and black-and-white illustrations. At the end of the book were a series of individual study questions, and Elner worked her way through the earlier chapters, especially (being half Italian) the Romans—along with illustrations—and presented these to Mr. Davison when she was deemed fit to return to school.

Generally speaking, life revolved around school and home. Not much else happened in life during Elner's junior school years. At Wolsingham, she and her classmates were expected to write a weekly diary while the dinner money was being added up. It was especially galling after school holidays when pupils were required to write "What I did on my holidays." Other people seemed to have gone somewhere at some point and done something. Stan had holidays, of course, but with his paired-off formerly motorbike gang. One summer, they went to North Wales, another time to the Isle of Man as Ralph Humble, one of the former "gang," was racing there. Stan painted a motif of a stag on his helmet using Elner's Bambi book to copy from an illustration.

After working at Redmires with Maurice for a while, Stan found a new job. Perhaps he had been encouraged to do so by Fred and Nelly, who were unhappy about his romantic attachment to Annie. For a while, Stan had to study surveying and similar skills at Darlington before being sent off to South Wales as a sales representative for Thomas Somerson, manufacturers of railway lines. In those days, coal mining was still an important industry, especially in South Wales, and replacing mineral line railways was necessary.

Stan was eventually also given a firm's car, although during his time in Wales, he still used Teapot. He also had a good salary, some of which had to be used for paying for digs in Chepstow during the week. He was also given a hospitality allowance for cigarettes and drinks for clients so that his personal smoking gradually increased to eighty cigarettes a day. Contrary to Fred and Nelly's plan, however, this change of work failed to part Stan and Annie. Every Friday, after work, Stan would drive back to Weardale, making the return trip to Wales on Monday mornings.

With regard to his responsibilities toward his parents and Elner, Stan dutifully made the occasional Saturday afternoon trip to Bishop Auckland or Darlington, usually to department stores or food shops. As Elner's feet kept growing, there were also visits to shoe shops when required. Elner was not happy about these. It was the custom back in these far-off days to try on the right shoe. If it felt comfortable and approved of by Nelly, then the left shoe was added for a quick circuit of the seating and the footwear duly purchased. When Elner later suffered blisters or sores to her left foot, this was her fault for not speaking up in the shoe shop. No one bothered to notice that the problems occurred with her left shoe, or that toe structures, foot sizes, and arch construction varied on the two feet. The left foot, for example, was bigger! Unlike most other females, Elner grew up with a dread hatred of shoe shops.

But it was not just the shoe shop that unsettled Elner about these shopping trips. It was the fact that Stan always passed a certain hotel at Witton-le-Wear on the return journey. This was supposed to be a family joke, but Elner never found it funny. At best, it was stupid; at worst (on shoe-shop trips), infuriating. "Shall we drop you off here, then?" the stupid adults would chuckle. She supposed it was their victory celebration for their "win" in the international "divorce versus Italy!" It was galling.

Another painful subject at her other extremity was her hairstyle. Back when Elner was six or seven and had wanted to grow her hair "to be like Janet Wilkinson," Nelly had said that if she wanted to grow it, it would have to stay long. She would not allow her to have it cut. However, Nelly came to regret that decision once she had had to deal with junior-school-aged Elner's plaits, which took more time the more they grew.

Poor Elner had to sit absolutely still for what felt like hours, while Nelly plaited away, sometimes pulling hard when she encountered "cotts," causing Elner to jump, causing Nelly to swipe her with the hairbrush. Fortunately, Elner had a hard head! Eventually, the hardness of it overcame the hairbrush, and it broke! So for a time, Nelly was reduced to using a comb. Torture over for the morning, Elner departed, ready for another day of having the blooming plaits pulled by schoolmates! Hair, like footwear, was a form of torture, except when playing cowboys and Indians, when she had a ready-made costume. She was always on the side of the indigenous North Americans even then. They seemed more like her than the cowboys did. When Nelly changed the tan-colored oilcloth chair seats for new red ones, Elner used a couple of the old ones to make herself an "Indian costume." She always enjoyed dressing up.

As regards her everyday clothes, these were often either second-hand or (in the case of cardigans, hats, scarves, mitts, and one particular dress made of hundred-year-old material) were Nelly made. On one occasion, though, Aunty Myra was having a lovely cream shantung silk dress made for Myrtle, with smocking on the bodice, so she had a beautiful green one in the same pattern made for Elner.

Considering the reduced circumstances that Nelly, Humphrey's eldest sister, now found herself in at a time of life when she should have been enjoying a comfortable work- and hassle-free retirement, Myra and Humphrey tried to make life easier for her. They bought her a television set and would sometimes take her, Fred, and Elner off for rides out in Humphrey's oh-so-smooth Mercedes car. The favorite place for such trips was the Lake District, stopping off at Hartside for coffee, toilets, and a chance for Fred to admire his panoramic view. He would point out the Solway Firth to Elner. "And that's Scotland on the other side of the water."

Then onward, to lakes and mountain passes, to Poet's Seat (where Fred told her about Wordsworth) or the Cataract of Lodore, followed up with stops for tea or to buy the obligatory tub of rum butter to take home. Fred, of course, pointed out the crosses on the mountains where climbers had slipped to their death. He also recounted how, when he was fit and young, at the end of the last century, he and a couple of other Frosterley lads cycled to the Lake District to gaze on all of this for the first time. Humphrey thought all this learning was fairly pointless. Business was what mattered; it produced money. What use was poetry?

Humphrey and Myra owned a caravan. For a time, it had been at Castle Douglas, but they now had moved it to Lochmaben to a peaceful place with only one other caravan beside a small loch inhabited by a family of swans. Shortly after Elner's hard head had ruined the hairbrush, reducing plait-making activities to comb only, Myra and Humphrey also announced that Nelly, Fred, and Elner deserved a holiday, or at least that Nelly and Fred deserved a holiday for looking after Elner! All three of them could go and stay for a week in the caravan in Scotland—a real week's holiday! Finally, she would have something to write in her school diary in September!

They explored Lochmaben and its shops itself first of all. Nelly, expert in both bread making and, formerly, bee keeping, bestowed her approval on both commodities. There were good broad beans and other vegetables too and some good mince to be had at the butchers. There was also a fish-and-chip shop.

The nearest towns were Lockerbie and Dumfries, so there were outings to both of these places. Most memorable in Dumfries was the marble statue of Robert Burns, yet another poet—the national poet of Scotland—who had written a poem about a mouse, which started off "wee, sleekit, cowrin, timrous beastie." Burns's pet dog was also sculpted at his feet on this fine Italian Carrara marble statue, but Fred and Elner walked around the back to see if the "mousie" was also there.

Shopping in Lockerbie, Nelly found the very thing she had been hunting for—no, certainly *not* a mouse! It was a new hairbrush with metal reinforcement. Had Elner known more of the mousie poem, she could have agreed on the prospect of this hairbrush find:

"But och! I backward cast my e'e.
On prospects drear!
An' forward; tho' I canna see,
I guess an' fear."

Apart from these two major excursions, the rest of the week was spent in Lochmaben. Elner sketched the swan family. She also sketched Stewart, from the next-door caravan, bravely feeding them. Elner was not prepared to go too near to them, though. She knew that a swan's wing could break a human's arm. She went on walks with Fred to find the other lochs of Lochmaben, while Nelly had her afternoon nap, and they noted the birds gathering along the telegraph wires, marking the end of summer and preparing for their long flight south to warmer lands.

Space was limited for Nelly's cooking endeavors, so Elner sat still on the bench that would be her sleeping place—later, reading.

She truly despaired of Myrtle's reading matter. Comics with teenage love stories were not her preferred reading, but she could compare the comics' agony aunts' solutions to the human condition with those of Nelly's women's magazines. Obviously, aging brought problems.

On returning to school as a third year junior, Elner discovered that, once again, she had Mrs. Morgan as her class teacher and that the class size had increased by half a dozen children. It had been decided to keep the least successful pupils from the class above in the third year juniors class for another year, enabling their fellows to progress more quickly with their eleven-plus studies. They were a somewhat bigger year group than any previously because they were born during '46 to '47, part of the wartime bulge.

This would also be the last year when there would be any senior-aged pupils in the county school. Wolsingham Grammar School was having a whole new modern (glass) structure built in a different field nearby. It would be ready to open as a secondary multilateral school in September 1958 as a huge complex with around a thousand pupils attending.

Elner found Mrs. Morgan much more friendly now. Some of the individual class projects were more interesting. Pupils were encouraged to work on their own on "poems I like" and "pets and garden creatures," both of which Elner enjoyed making.

Sadly, this was around the time when Elner's cat Blossom died. Elner returned from school to learn of this tragedy. "What did she die of, Nonna?"

"Mortification"

"What's that?"

"Well, she was going to have kittens, but they got stuck inside her, and the vet couldn't do anything about it."

"Oh."

Elner drew a sad portrait of Blossom in her "my pets" book. Billy, her Stanhope Show goldfish had also been short-lived. Thus, Elner turned her concentration to the garden creatures section, having lost both pets.

Her third-year class were given a specialist teacher from the seniors, Miss Errington, to take their art lessons. Miss Errington, as a young teacher, had taught art to Stan when he was in the higher tops, and she was very encouraging of Elner's artistic efforts. One of the set books that year was *Treasure Island*, and Miss Errington and Mrs. Morgan both admired Elner's depiction of some of the characters. She had, in fact, given them real character.

During autumn '57, while Stan was still studying surveying and before he disappeared to South Wales in "Rippy," it was decided to take a trip to Blackpool Illuminations in Teapot. Fred and Stan sat in the front, Nelly and Annie on the back seat, and Elner was given a cushion in the luggage area, which was devoid of any backrest.

The thought of these famous illuminations should have been thrilling for a nine-year-old, but it was a long, uncomfortable journey in a cramped space. The chance to stretch her legs would have been welcome! Eventually, they arrived and drove along, watching the wonderful sights. Then, replete with man-made phenomena, they turned for home. Elner felt worse and worse. Her throat was very sore, and her head ached. She tried to lie down comfortably but ached all over, and she was cold!

Finally, the torment of the long homeward journey ended. Elner was given an aspirin and put to bed with a hot-water bottle. The Asian flu epidemic had arrived in Stanhope. It arrived at around the same time that the nuclear accident at Seascale happened some distance north of Blackpool and to the southwest of Weardale, the prevailing winds in that part of the country also being southwesterlies. The fire started at Seascale on the tenth of October in a complex then being used for making hydrogen bombs. The Cold War was alive and well back then. The fire burned for three days, with radioactive fallout blown across the North Sea and into parts of Europe. So Elner's adults visit to the illuminations on Saturday, October 12, was not the best of decisions really. Seascale was a level 5 nuclear accident—the worst there has ever been in the UK. For Elner's schoolfellows, there was no school milk for a time, and the words "strontium 90" came into everyday use.

Having recovered from Asian flu, Elner arrived at her tenth birthday. "Oh, you're growing up! You're in double figures now," said the grown-ups perkily.

They were surprised when Elner burst into tears. "But I don't want to grow up," she objected, gazing at the proof of such insanity—her adults. "I want to be a child forever, like Peter Pan."

Chapter 8

For around two years after leaving St. John's Chapel, Elner was sometimes allowed to invite former school friends to come to Stanhope and play on Saturdays. Not all together, of course! Sometimes, Barbara and Sheila Scott visited. On other occasions, Janet Wilkinson would travel from Crook, where she now lived, sometimes with Mrs. Wilkinson and sometimes on her own. They would play cowboys and Indians, dressing up, or ballet schools. Janet and Elner also rode around on pretend horses or watched show jumping on the television.

There were reciprocal visits too. Elner would go to Crook by bus. Janet would meet her at the marketplace, and they would wend their way along Hope Street to the railway. There, they would climb up the pedestrian bridge and look out for steam trains passing by underneath them. Then on, they went to 41 High Hope Street, where Janet, David, and Madge, their mother, lived. David was a big boy now, hoping to join the navy when he was old enough. He had a bird-egg collection and model planes.

One Saturday, after arriving at Crook, Elner travelled on with the Wilkinsons to Durham for the adventure of seeing the impressive cathedral and then having a picnic down by the river. A tree had been washed in from previous flooding, so Janet and Elner pretended it was a dragon.

Elner was envious of friends with siblings. It must be fun, she mused, to wake up in a house with other people of a similar age. When she was allowed friends for the Saturday, she was so happy that she wished the visit could go on and on. When no one was looking, she would hide a friend's coat or bag in the hope that they would miss the last bus and have to stay at Stanhope!

Sadly, after several last-minute hunts, Nelly decided she was too old for such nonsense. How could she stop the friends' visits? Well, she decided, Elner was…constipated, and Saturday, of course, was the only day when she could force her to take laxatives as there was school on weekdays and Sunday school on Sundays. First of all, she inflicted the disgusting senna tea on Elner. Perhaps it was Myra who suggested that chocolate laxatives existed? But it too had an unpleasantly nonchocolate taste. There followed something called Seidlitz powder. Well, at least it was effervescent.

Poor Elner. Social life, as other children knew it, was ruined by Nelly's masterstroke. She spent Saturdays within close proximity of the lavatory or "the closet" (as Fred called it) from then on until she learned enough to inform Nelly that her digestive system was actually being ruined by these artificial measures and needed to reassert its natural rhythms. But by then, there was no social life anymore. Saturday had become weekend homework day!

To make up for the lack of social life, Elner was finally allowed to take piano lessons (now that she no longer craved them). The piano teacher, Amy Potts, lived almost directly across the road from Elner. She was a friend of Margaret Currah and the sister of Mrs. Irene Bainbridge, who taught English at the grammar school. Elner remembered the three young women—Amy, Irene, and Margaret—as they were then swinging her between them over the hay rows up the back field one evening, when Nelly and Fred were still living at Ward's Villa and the Currahs at Parson Byers, with its angry guard goose called Jock.

Elner's piano lessons took place in Amy's front room, which contained large beautifully decorated vases and urns. The Potts family were originally from Sunderland, and Amy's father had been a sea captain, who brought these ceramics back to her mother from faraway places. Some were about a yard high! Elner enjoyed the actual lessons and progressed well, but her grown-ups caused her difficulties, as usual. They fixed it so that her lessons were the same day and time as her favorite television program. Sadly, it was also the day when the fishman called, and Nelly would insist on buying kippers to cook for tea. Poor Elner felt inhibited—nay, embarrassed—during piano lessons in such an elegant vase-filled room, when she was affected by the clinging kipper smell!

During the week, she was also made to do half an hour's piano practice a day at home. Fred's piano lived in the sitting room. This was not a problem in summer, but winter was a dank chilly matter in that unused room, where the fire was only lit for Christmas and New Year. At times, she complained that her hands were too cold, so the grown-ups allowed her a one-bar electric fire, only to be turned on when the lesson started! By the end of the lesson, it was almost usefully lukewarm!

Because Elner was showing some promise, Amy mentioned grade exams. "Oh, no," said Fred. "She should just learn to enjoy playing." (But perhaps the grades would have given Elner incentive and a measure of her progress.)

Soon after Elner started piano lessons, Amy had a concert for her pupils "upstairs at the store," where Elner had once—and clumsily—taken ballet lessons. Wanting to encourage Elner, although her playing had only just started, Amy tested her singing and suggested she could sing "All through the Night." Elner was really pleased. It was a Welsh song, and her daddy worked in Wales too—but...

"No," said Fred, the family expert on musical matters, and that was that. Elner was allowed only to attend and watch other children taking part.

Stan was actually not in Wales for much longer, though. Instead, he was transferred—"sent to Coventry" (with great family joking involved). His new area was the Midlands. He found digs, centrally at Keresley, travelling from the Welsh border in the west to the Wash in the east. He had a new Austin A35 too, with a North Yorkshire plate number RPY 44 ("Rippy") instead of the local (Bishop Auckland) "PT" registration.

Meanwhile, Elner's position in Mrs. Morgan's class was improving. She was third at Christmas and second at the end of the year. The classroom had a nature table, with both tadpoles and caterpillars going through their life cycles there, except, of course, that no one

thought to put some sort of mesh over the tank containing the tadpoles with growing legs! On return to school one Monday morning,
the class was amused to discover a school populated, it seemed, by a
plague of minifrogs!

So when it came to the time for butterflies to break out from
chrysalises and fly away, Elner was chosen to take their glass-sided
container out to the headmaster's garden and observe their release.
She had, after all, been the one to catch the caterpillars, having no
squeamishness about creepy-crawlies. She found Stan's fear of spiders
strangely amusing.

School holidays arrived, and during the holidays, Stan's landlady
absented herself from his digs for a week. This was a good opportunity, then, for Nelly to enjoy "a few days' peace" by sending Fred and
Elner to Coventry as well! Their first stop was to watch Lady Godiva
on horseback ride round the clock at 7:00 p.m.

Next day, Fred was keen to visit the Shakespeare places at
Stratford, so off they went to his home in Stratford and also to

Ann Hathaway's cottage in Shottery. Elner was really taken by this thatched cottage. There were no thatched buildings in Weardale. Even Stanhope Hall and the Norman Stone houses had stone, not thatched, roofs.

They returned to the car to head back to Keresley, then a strange thing happened. They were in Rippy, driving along a country lane, when another motorist pursued them, hooting and flashing lights. Stan looked in his rearview mirror and tried to ignore the other car. But then it overtook them, and the woman motorist waved at them to stop!

No, there was nothing wrong with Rippy, except its number plate—its Yorkshire number plate. But the lady driver, originally from the North Riding, was apparently already well acquainted with Stan and was now interested to meet Stan's father and daughter. "Come home with me and have tea," she invited them. It would have been churlish to refuse, so the embarrassed Stan followed her home, father and daughter in tow.

When they arrived, three children ran out to meet them, asking their mother if they could make toffee on the cooker. Remarkably (as Elner saw such things from a Nelly perspective), this mother actually allowed them free range to "play" with the kitchen utensils and the ingredients, and Elner was welcome to join in with this toffee-making game, while the adults chatted. They were nice, friendly children, and this was all good, chaotic fun.

They drove back to Keresley. Next day, Stan's work took him in the opposite direction, heading toward the east coast. They stayed the night in a pub belonging to someone called Aubrey, originally from Weardale. It was on a quiet road in flat countryside. Next day, Stan made calls at Wisbech and King's Lynn for work, but there was no stopping to take in places of interest along the way. Apart from the Shakespeare places, the toffee making, the Lady Godiva clock, and a spot of fresh air on King's Lynn docks, there wasn't much else to say about this "holiday outing." Any trips with Stan "on duty" usually meant sitting in the car outside an office, factory, or work site, with precious little in the way of scenery to admire.

During this school summer holiday, though, Nelly was visited by two of her old former Stanhope friends—Madge and Will

Snowball. Madge and Will had had two children back then, a boy called Robin and a girl called Sybil. Age wise, they were contemporaries of Maurice and Stan. Sybil was married and lived at Marton near Middlesbrough across the Tees from Billingham, where Will, approaching retirement, now had a chemist's shop. Like Fred and Nelly, there was a difference of six years between Madge and Will, but the other was round—Madge was Fred's age and Will was Nelly's. Even so, Madge invited Elner to stay with them during the October half-term holiday to give Nelly (or Elner?) a break. (At least, Myra had persuaded Nelly to allow Elner to have her hair cut short a week or two beforehand, so there was no early morning hair battle now.)

During that week in Billingham, Madge and Elner crossed the Tees on the transporter bridge—exciting in itself—but went on to visit the museum at Middlesbrough. Elner had never been to a museum before and found the place very interesting, except...in the last room were skulls and skeletons. Elner did *not* want to see them. She could not explain why. There was only a feeling of dread about the thought of them.

Madge was understanding and let this be, apart from pointing out that the skeletons, including the human one, were very interesting. On another day, they met Madge's granddaughters Carol and Hilary. Carol was around Myrtle's age, while Hilary was a year younger than Elner but looked older. Elner stayed at their house for one night, meeting their pets—Coco and Pepe the poodles, rabbits, budgies—and learning that they also had two ponies out in a field somewhere with a view of Roseberry Topping. Hilary and Elner took the poodles across the road for a walk in the park. They agreed to write to each other, and Elner was invited back next summer.

Soon after the October weekend came Bonfire Night. The Scotts had made a big bonfire, and Elner was invited. As it was dark, Nelly agreed to come with her. But as soon as they got off the bus, Nelly told Elner, "Off you go then."

"But you said you'd come with me. It's dark."

"Well, here's a torch, then. I'm going to Mrs. Peart's to wait for you."

So Elner had to trudge along the lane, over the disused railway, a field, the white bridge over the river, and two more fields on her own in the dark, with a fairly useless torch. The final field contained fairly obvious cow statues. At least, Elner hoped against hope, that all the cattle were female, although the night was so black that no bull would have noticed a red rag or a royal blue duffle coat, come to that! She made it to the bonfire, enjoyed the evening, and the Scott youngsters, with big boy Peter in charge, set her back to civilization and Nelly.

Elner was now in the "scholarship" year at school, with lots of homework, in preparation for the eleven-plus exam. She was also in the top class, as all secondary-age children were now at the multi-lateral complex. So her class were rotaed as porch monitors, dealing with crying smaller kids with playground scraps and scrapes, applying Dettol and if necessary, Elastoplast. They also made sure the towel bags were on the right pegs and supervised classes exiting in file from assembly, just like the fourteen-year-olds had done in previous years.

It was also, in Nelly's eyes, for a granddaughter almost as tall as she was, a time to put away childish things. There was that scruffy old rag doll Betty for a start. "You're a big girl, and you still play with that tatty old thing. I'm sure you love that blooming doll more than you love me, in spite of all I do for you, slaving away."

"No, I don't, Nonna."

"Oh, yes, you do!"

And Nelly kept up this banter until Elner ended up heartbroken but tearless, putting her beloved rag doll on the fire to prove to Nelly that Betty was not a rival for her grandmother's affections.

Nelly was also fighting a grudge match with "those Eyeties"— namely, Elner's other set of grandparents, Antonio and Maria, in Italy, whom she had never met. They had both worked as teachers, so it was important to prove to them that Elner could "get on in life" just as well without them. It was also important to "get Elner through for the grammar school" because, unlike Judith, Billy, and Myrtle, she would not be able to transfer to private education if she failed. Because life was real and earnest now, Elner's piano lessons were cancelled.

Uncle Maurice, who had done "maths exams at Cambridge University" in order to be a pilot, came to the rescue in the "we are not doing coaching" stakes. He would call in on his way home from work and, along with his parents, would turn the maths "problems" into a competition. Which of the four of them could work out the correct answer first?

The English questions required knowledge of who wrote which famous books, alongside comprehension questions and other such things. The class was given old maths and English papers from previous years' first rounds of the eleven-plus for homework. Those who were lucky enough to pass the first part would later be called upon to sit the second part in the new year at the New School.

It was often the custom to give a successful scholarship candidate a new bike back in those days. Elner was still riding around on Myrtle's little blue bike from the Christmas when she was eight. She really needed a bicycle, which allowed her knees space to move without contact with the handlebars. Someone she knew already had a pink and purple flashy, with a three-speed and fancy handlebars— the latest fashion in bicycles. Elner, though, would have happily settled for a new but ordinary red bike.

However, when Christmas arrived, lo and behold, there stood…a seven-year-old blue secondhand bicycle. "I don't believe in bribing children with bicycles when they pass exams. I'm assuming you'll pass, so here's a bike for you now as a Christmas present."

Well, it was the right size, after all! But what was his real reason for the early present? Had the bike been advertised at a reasonable price, or was he saving up for something more important in his eyes? Time would tell.

Now came the scholarship exam term. Elner passed the first part. With wonderful timing, Nelly had organized for Elner to have a polio injection the evening before the exam. (Yes, an injection. There were three in all in those days before the easy sugar-lump option.) There had been an outbreak of polio at Stanhope, and Kay Hobson next door was currently in an iron lung.

On returning from the injection, Nelly suggested that Elner should go to bed early. Sadly, this coincided with a power cut, so

Elner couldn't even read in bed to take her mind off things. Next morning, she caught a special bus for the examinees and walked from the school bus parking area up the path to the glassy new school, glittering in the sunlight. From there, the children were taken to the exam room for the numerical reasoning. After that, there was a break. Then came the verbal reasoning paper. Elner zipped her way through it, then checked her answers.

Strange, she thought. *Why does this exam have 105 questions?*

She watched the others hard at work. She asked to go to the toilet, mainly to relieve the boredom. Finally, pens down and papers collected. Elner walked back to the J. M. & I School with Valerie Stirling, Sylvia Hossack, David Brown, Ian Littlewood, Robert Carson (a new boy that year, who was from Harperley Police Training near Fir Tree), and one or two others. "What was your answer for question 115?" Valerie asked Elner.

"There wasn't a 115," Elner replied, puzzled.

"Yes, there was. On the very back!"

Drat. The examiners had put questions on the outside of the back cover—fifteen of the blooming things! At that rate, she would probably have failed, she imagined...gloomily. Remarkably, though, she had passed anyway. She would be in the Grammar School Stream after all! And while the other successful kids were feted one way or another by proud parents, Stan gave Elner a box of chocolates. "You already have your bike. Children should not be given bribes for passing exams."

So Elner departed primary education with a presentation copy of *Wuthering Heights*. School holidays started, and Elner was sitting in Stan's car, while he stood outside Archibald's ironmongers, gazing up at Annie, peering out from her staff bedroom attached to Stanhope Castle Approved School.

It was the usual Romeo and Juliet scene, but Elner picked up the words "Bishop Auckland," "registrar," and "a lot of controversy." Returning home and eventually catching Nelly alone, she announced, "I think they're planning to get married." Indeed, they were. So that was why he was saving up; nothing whatever to do with an antibribing offspring campaign!

If they had kept their promise about allowing her to be a bridesmaid, perhaps she could have forgiven them. But, no. Stan wanted Ralph Humble, not big brother Maurice, as his best man. So Annie asked Judith to be the adult bridesmaid and the four-year-old of some obscure cousin or friend to be the "small" bridesmaid. The venue was the rather dour Wearhead Chapel, with refreshments and viewing of presents afterward. Elner wore a coffee-colored dress with small white dots (secondhand from Myrtle). She spent the service feeling very angry with the Methodist Church for agreeing to the validity of the union. "Never mind," Nelly had told her. "She doesn't want you, so you are safe with us."

It was toward the end of August when the wedding took place. The "happy couple" was moving to Coventry, Annie having found a deputy cook post in a technical college.

Elner, meanwhile, had her new school uniform to take her mind off harsher realities. Unbelievably too, on her first day at her new school (though in the "old" 1912 building), she was surprised that despite having missed so many questions in the second exam, she found herself in a higher grammar stream form than Valerie Stirling.

Unbelievably too, she, a Stanhoper, won first prize for art at Wolsingham Show on the first Saturday in September, with a picture of someone show jumping. Stan was still around that weekend and took her to see the picture with its red ticket in the produce tent, then she had a photo taken with a monkey on her shoulder as a new chapter began.

Chapter 9

The first year at the new school was fine. Elner's form was out in the peaceful prefab classrooms, behind the "old" school building. She found her classmates friendly and worked so hard that at the end of the year, she was promoted to the A form. The grammar stream—in England, this means secondary-aged youngsters bright enough to have passed both parts of the eleven-plus—consisted of forms A, B, and C. D form contained those who had passed the first half of the eleven-plus, and the rest were in forms E, F, and G. Transfer was possible, both up or down if necessary. The year above, the bigger wartime-bulge year, even had a form H. This cannot have helped the confidence of those in H.

In a sense, the whole thing was a mean, competitive system, which discouraged rather than encouraged. The school was out to prove a point, both as one of the entries in the later book *Comprehensive Experiment* (although, strictly speaking, it wasn't comprehensive at all) and also in the county's O and A level league tables.

Elner went to stay with Carol and Hilary during the October holidays of her first form year. They visited a Chinese restaurant, where Elner hadn't a clue what to order so ended up with omelet, although not keen on eggs. This was probably the first time she had set foot in a restaurant. She rode one of the ponies and was complimented on having "a good seat" (no doubt from riding Antony's skewbald bareback along a stony lane a couple of years ago, with the boys trying to make her fall off). But there was an atmosphere to the place now, the early rounds of parents splitting up—something remembered from infancy, perhaps.

Madge and Will had retired, moved from the chemist's shop and were now living in a small bungalow by the sea at Marske. She and Hilary went to visit them. Standing alone on one of the sand dunes there, Elner was suddenly struck by the realization that she would die one day, that all this would end. Was it surprising then that things started falling apart during her second and third form years?

Remarkably, during this time, a small change gave an alternative stability for a time. The other Madge—Madge Wilkinson, the mother of Janet—came back into her life for a time because Myra was sending Myrtle to elocution lessons after school at the home of a Mrs. Crinson of "Lanercost," Wolsingham. Elner was informed that she was to learn elocution too. Her school friend Vivienne Carter, who lived a few doors away from the Crinsons, was also going. So for a time. Elner would walk to Vivienne's after school, eat a lovely tea there (with "bought cakes"—never allowed by Nelly), and then go up the lane to "Lanercost" to drown in the joys of poetry.

Elner picked up a certificate and two medals issued by the Poetry Society—but, more importantly, an increased love of the joy of poetic language, which had started with the hymns and prayers book years before. There was sometimes a sense of beauty, stability, and encompassing, of the Word beyond the words.

But the "home" pattern was changing. Nelly and Fred were growing older. Stan and Annie had a new life in Coventry, setting up home together, driving around with furniture on the roof rack, and making new friends.

Nelly, meanwhile, found herself torn hither and thither. She had always been one of those village women who took on the roles of Terry Pratchett's witches—tending the sick, lancing boils, laying out the dead, talking to the bees she had kept at Ward's Villa. In fact, Elner would reflect in later life, it was rather like being brought up by Granny Weatherwax but without the magic, only with the attitude!

Aunty Mame, Nelly's younger sister, was married to Tom Mews, who had farmed the Stanhope Hall land for years. When their son Harry needed a boil lancing or a hen ploating and preparing for cooking, he would come, not to his mother, but to her big sister.

Once, he brought a hen that had still been in full egg production, and Nelly removed the unnecessary and inedible interior; there were eggs in various stages of formation. Perhaps that was why Elner was not keen on eggs.

Tom Mews, like Aunty's husband, Wilf, had survived the First World War, including the gas, at the time. Now, the long-term effects of gassing came back to haunt both of them. So Nelly was called upon to support Aunty Mame with Tom's overnight nursing so that someone was always there, either to call ambulance or doctor or to be there with him at the end.

After Tom died, Aunty Mame took ill, so Nelly was called upon for another stint of nursing. Aunty Mame suffered a stroke, losing the use of one arm and the power to communicate coherently. Elner realized the poor woman was still perfectly in her right mind and felt annoyed that some others could not understand this and began talking down to her because of her attempts at speech.

Wilf Philipson, Aunty's husband, also died around this time. The memorial service was in Bridge End Chapel, Frosterley, on an Easter Sunday evening, with a reading and sermon about the road to Emmaus. This was the chapel where Fred's father had been organist and choirmaster for many years, and there was a stained glass window in memory of him and his wife.

With her duties of helping other family members, as well as her job at the lodge, Nelly was feeling worn out. The car park light had not been working, and none of the masons had bothered to fix it before lodge night. Zipping across the dark yard from lodge to home, Nelly tripped over planks or the coke heap in the dark. Elner was woken, alarmed by Nelly, arm in plaster, arriving late to bed in the dark.

Not long afterward, Elner had another shock when Nelly woke up one morning horror-struck, almost blind! Nelly felt her way noisily and in fearful panic along the passage wall to the bathroom, where she splashed cold water on her face. This prompt action apparently saved the sight in one eye, a specialist told her later. He gave her strict instructions about not using salt in her cooking and not straining the good eye with knitting and sewing.

After attempting food without salt, Nelly ignored the warning. For the years she had left, she would enjoy what she ate, she protested. She also saw the specialist's instructions regarding sewing and knitting as a rule to be gotten around. She took up crocheting instead, even though that caused her greater eyestrain than either of the other activities. Old age did not mellow her; it made her more devious.

Stan and Annie, meanwhile, were making new friends in Coventry. There was one young man in particular by the name of Barry. He was a rugby player, an excellent swimmer, and popular with the girls. Annie was most impressed because one of his girlfriends was a beauty queen. Barry and his girlfriend came to visit Weardale on one of the rare Weardale weeks that could pass for summer. The Humble lads had dammed back Killhope Burn in a spot on their land so that it was deep enough for swimming.

Stan was also a good swimmer, having swum as a soldier both competitively and, more importantly, to survive in wartime, swimming out to safety in the British withdrawal from the Cretan coast. Since Elner had been saved from drowning by Barbara Scott, she was wary of water and did not trust Stan teaching her. But Barry Proctor, a trained swimming coach in addition to his rugby activities, made the time to teach her how to swim.

On one visit to the pool, Elner noticed something strange about her wet footprints on the smoother rocks. They could have been made by two different humans, judging by their shapes. The left foot was flat while the right was slightly smaller with a high arch. How odd! And no one had ever noticed this before.

Barry returned some time later with a different girlfriend, who did not meet with Nelly's approval. She (a town lass used to man-made urban pools), sadly, jumped straight out into the water from the small waterfall and slashed her leg open on a sharp rock. That ended the swimming for the day. Instead, there was a mad car chase from one dale's doctor to another, with the nearest, at Westgate, saying he was off duty. Bishop Auckland Hospital, well over thirty miles away, was probably the nearest A and E; but fortunately, the leg was dealt with at Stanhope Surgery, and the girl was shocked but fine.

However, Stan's time in Coventry came to an end before long, when he was transferred to the London office in 5a, Dean's Yard, Westminster. Annie had no intentions of living in London, so she returned to her mother's house in Wearhead and her old job at Stanhope Castle. Stan found a landlady in Hampstead, and off he went to work in "Swinging Sixties' London." At weekends, he slept at Mrs. Wall's and visited his mother and father from there.

Aunty Myra had a cat, which had produced two white kittens, one fluffy and one plain. Elner could have one. She chose the plain one and called him Pandy. Nelly insisted that he slept in the coal house—not the best accommodation for a white kitten.

As he grew older, he began to stray across neighbors' gardens. At sunset, Nelly would dispatch Elner to retrieve the erring feline, who gradually turned into a tomcat. At least, in the back gardens, he was safe, although annoying to others. But one day, he followed Elner, who had gone to the shop over the road. She came out, carrying her purchase, only to see her cat lying dead in the road. "Bookie Joe" was passing and kindly moved the corpse onto the pavement, where it could be retrieved and buried, not crushed. Elner wept bitterly at the loss of Pandy.

Perhaps this incident reminded her of when, a few years earlier, a speeding motorist squealed to a halt when Nelly was making that crossing. He berated Nelly for being a stupid old woman. Elner had wanted to punch the idiot man and tell him not to bully her grandmother but instead comforted her hurt authority figure. With Pandy's demise, she could let her emotions flow.

Nelly rarely went anywhere, although remarking often enough that, when her ship came in, she would visit all her relatives in Vancouver. One of them, Delma, and her husband, Clark, were in London for a year while Clark attended an art course. They met up with Stan, who brought them north to visit Nelly from time to time.

As Stan was now based in London, Nelly came to the conclusion that she should catch up with another old friend, one on her Christmas cake list—a Mrs. Roberts in Whitstable, whose husband had been in charge of the German prisoners, who worked in Fred's quarry in the First World War. Nelly decided that Stan could take her to Whitstable and that she and Elner could take a look at London as they passed through. Back in the '60s, it was possible for Stan to park his latest firm's car *in* Dean's Yard, leaving Nelly and Elner to sit in the car, watching the choirboys playing cricket.

But the Whitstable trip was a rather sad and sorry affair. Nelly, who fussed about cleanliness, discovered her old friend living alone in an isolated wooden bungalow that was full of flies and bluebottles. However, Nelly stayed the night there, as previously agreed, while Stan and Elner found rooms in a B&B and a meal of sole and chips at a local chippy.

Next morning, they travelled to the Isle of Sheppey. Elner had fancifully imagined a wild island from the times of Hengist and Horsa. Instead, she found herself all alone in a parked car for hours outside the extremely smelly glue factory! Ah, the mystic glamor of London and the sarf. (Some years later, on an October week to "Swinging London" with Stan, she spent an entire afternoon parked in a gloomy side street outside Battersea power station. Oh, if only it had been a modern art gallery back then, needing railway lines for an immense installation on the rage of the trained, the single-track life, or some such event!)

A very saddened Nelly was eventually rescued from the fly-filled bungalow. They returned to London, with Stan visiting the office once more. This time, Elner was dispatched to "go and have a look around Westminster Abbey" on her own, while Nelly snoozed in the car. When Stan had finished work, he took photos of Nelly and Elner in Dean's Yard and of Elner with Westminster Abbey and Big Ben in the background. The only highlight of the journey home was strawberry ice cream soda, a unique experience of a beverage, which never reached Weardale!

After this summer trip, Elner went into the third form. Those in 3A were placed on the top floor at the western end of the north-facing slope of the glass building. Beyond the hockey pitch, there was a sunny hill with trees and fields. Elner tended to focus more attention on that than she did on the blackboard of a bleak functional classroom, which became progressively colder as winter approached. Those in 3B had the sunny overheated room next door. Down a floor, 4A and B had their classrooms across the landing from the chem lab, from which unpleasant aromas all too frequently arose.

Elner had been finding science subjects increasingly pointless because none of the science teachers explained the reason behind their subjects. Chemistry was particularly annoying. It was about mixing substance A with substance B in order to produce an invisible gas and a scattering of crystals, a sort of magic trick without a white rabbit. No one ever explained what the substances were, where they came from, or how they were extracted. They just were. The same applied to the end products and the periodic table. Chemistry was only enlivened by having Megan Jones as a partner for the experiments. They never followed the prescribed recipes.

The same irrelevance criticism was true of physics. *Why* mess about with magnets and iron filings or the workings of artesian wells? Why not study astrophysics instead? And as for years of biology exams involving spirogyra, amoeba, and hydra…please, couldn't we study natural history or medicine, which fitted better into Elner's concept of real life? Science, as dished out in the third form, bored her silly. Although Fred had explained artesian wells to her the year before, he was no longer all that helpful. Perhaps he was ailing. One day, there was some family joke about going to heaven, with Elner pulling Fred's leg, "No, you'll go to the other place." It was just a joke.

With no art mark to up her scores, and German grammar even more complex than Latin (and no one to help with rote learning), she began to flounder. Her classmates were turning into teenagers. The girls were suddenly silly, giggly, and boy daft, while the boys were turning into loutish aliens from another planet. Her acne flourished, and her health was not good either. Just in time to miss the Christmas party, she caught flu. Fred was ill at the same time, bothered once again by duodenal ulcers, being cared for and cosseted.

Fred's seventy-ninth birthday happened with the winter solstice, and he had various visitors that day, bringing greetings to him in the warm bedroom at the top of the stairs. Elner, infectiously fluey, was stranded in solitary state all day long in the far cold bedroom, feeling peeved and lonely. She went to the bathroom to clean her teeth, but, jealous of all Fred's attention, she never bothered to say good night to him and fell into a deep sleep.

Waking late the next morning—the twenty-second—she heard Uncle Maurice's voice speaking into the phone on the staircase. "Hello. Mr. Clark? This is Maurice Makepeace. My father died earlier this morning. I was ringing to ask if you could take the funeral?"

She got out of bed, pulled on Nelly's ancient red dressing gown, and headed downstairs to a living room full of relatives, now panicking at the sight of her because someone (*else*, each was thinking) would have to break the news. Looking at them, she said, "It's all right. I know. I heard Uncle Maurice on the phone to Mr. Clark."

They had all gone to the hospital after Fred had hemorrhaged during the night. Stan had driven up full pelt from London but had somewhere or how acquired Annie along the way. Fred had ignored her, so Stan was feeling hurt. Maurice and Jessie had been there too. Elner had been left alone all night in the house. Just as well, in a way, that she had not woken up, but she was guilt-ridden that she had never said good night. Nelly was inconsolable. Though the family "boss," she was lost without her Fred.

The funeral was set for Christmas Eve at 2:30 p.m. in High Street Methodist Church, with interment afterward in Stanhope Cemetery and a funeral tea at Nelly's afterward. It would be taken by Mr. Clark, the Westgate minister, as Fred and the Stanhope minister had not been on good terms. Besides, Mr. Clark lived just a field away from Maurice and Jessie—currently residing at Westgate—and Judith was involved in youth work for him.

The relatives departed, and Elner was left to console Nelly. Elner's flu was forgotten about.

On the evening of the twenty-third, having spent most of the day with her mourning grandmother while others came and went, Elner felt that she just had to get out of the house. Stan was going off on a "Wall" errand, collecting Annie's sister Jean from Barrow-in-Furness. Jean's husband was working on a submarine in the far north of Scotland, so Jean was spending Christmas with her Wearhead family. Elner asked to go on the journey, relishing the cold bleak fells outside before the return to duty.

She had wanted to attend the funeral but had no black coat. Annie came up with (Lilian's?) thin dark blue summer raincoat. But even Elner's school gaberdine was slightly darker and warmer and also totally unsuitable for someone with flu at a time when the ground was ice solid with a hard frost. She was sent to Stanhope Hall for the duration of the funeral and taken back home for the tea.

Next day, Christmas Day, she and Nelly went to Maurice and Jessie's home. Stan and Annie were at Wearhead with the Walls. It was the end of the family unit that Elner had known. And all the time, Elner was feeling so guilty. Not only had she not said goodbye to Fred, she was unable to cry. How was that possible when she had wept copious tears for little cat Pandy? What sort of human being was she?

One night, she had a dream. She was sitting in the little chair by the fire when Fred, looking old and drawn, walked into the living room and put his hands on the pull-down door of the area above the fireplace, where bread rose, sticks for the fire dried, or plates could be warmed. Fred stood, hands rested there, and said, "How black is hell."

Glaring white snow came straight after Christmas. Elner, well or not, went out with her shovel and wellies, digging paths for Nelly to the coal house and lodge kitchen, for Mrs. Wearmouth the postwoman, and anyone else coming to the back door.

It was a fortnight before the tears would come. Time to return to school by then and feel lost and numb there as well.

Chapter 10

"A disappointing result. She will have to work hard to recover lost ground." Thus spoke the headmaster.

After Fred's death, Elner felt herself floundering. She was alone with Nelly now, but Nelly wanted to follow Fred. Every night, after Elner went up to bed, Nelly would rake the fire out. While the cinders in the grate cooled, she would talk to Fred's chair. Every night, the same—she would talk to her Fred. Elner could hear her all the way to the far bedroom. Then Nelly would set the fire for morning and make her way upstairs to her black bullets and magazines and prewarmed bed, and one night, she arrived with a bleeding brow. Somehow, she'd hurt herself setting the fire.

Elner had asked if she could have Fred's bedroom for herself now as there were just the two of them living in the house. After all, when Stan returned to Weardale from London at weekends, he generally stayed at Wearhead with his wife in Mrs. Wall's house.

But Nelly was not prepared to let Elner have a warmer room of her own for study, despite Mr. Dand's instructions to all of the A stream that they needed a quiet space of their own to work in. No. Nelly argued that sometimes—she did not add, "When they have overindulged at the Grey Bull"—Stan and Annie would be able to stay at her house on a Saturday night. Thus, she could have her son around the house on Sunday mornings. Otherwise, when would she see him? So Elner continued the nightly homework task, sitting on the mat in front of the fire, books spread around her, writing on her lap, while Nelly crocheted, cigarette dangling from the corner of her mouth, with her television keeping up a stream of distracting conversation or ad jingles.

During the Easter term following Fred's death, there were marks for classwork and tests, rather than exams, and there was a likeable young man student for English and German. So for a term, she rallied, and her schoolwork was back to its usual standard. But summer term brought a new slump. Her school report said that she should do better, that she lacked concentration. But which of those teachers considered her home conditions and worrying lack of stability?

There was a nice older boy, whose name was Michael Raisbeck. His mother had died some years before, and he lived with his father. One morning, the Stanhope school bus did not leave at its usual time; it stood waiting. Somehow, news gradually percolated to the pupils that they were waiting for Michael. Eventually, he arrived, and the journey began. Apparently, Michael had gotten up for school, and not hearing his dad up and about for work, had gone to waken him only to find him unresponsive—dead. Michael phoned the police and the doctor. They told the school bus to wait, informed the school and relatives, then sent Michael off to school. Life (or dealing with death) was like that then. Eventually, Michael was dispatched to relatives in Australia and "did well for himself" in Aussie academia.

But because of this incident, the fear was placed in Elner's mind that one morning, she could wake up to find Nelly lying beside her in the same bed dead. After all, Nelly was much older than Michael's father had been. Elner remembered the morning when Nelly had woken up blind! Moreover, Nelly actually wanted to die and join Fred! If Nelly died, what would happen to her? Stan was working in London, living in digs during the week and mainly, otherwise, in the Wall's council house at Wearhead (to Nelly's disapproval).

Without Fred around the house, the morning routine changed. Nelly, as always, liked to have a lie-in. She would set the alarm clock (always five blooming minutes fast!) and then: "Elner, Elner, get up! It's quarter past seven." (Add to this the fact that it was really only ten past seven, and Elner knew it was. This was not the sort of thing most fourteen-year-olds want to hear, anyway.)

Elner would wander to the bathroom, get washed, and clean her teeth with pink Euthymol. Sometimes, she used to attempt to sing to start the day well until Nelly assured her that singing before breakfast was extremely unlucky. She would put on her uniform, light the fire, set the fireguard, sprint to the paper shop, collect the *Northern Echo*, return home, make Nelly's morning cup of tea, and then take it upstairs, along with the *Northern Echo*. After all of that, she could chomp on her Sugar Puffs or cornflakes while listening to the Home Service.

One morning an educational psychologist was being interviewed about his latest book in which he propounded that maternal deprivation at an early age was a contributory factor to juvenile delinquency. "Huh," said Elner. "I'm not going to be a juvenile delinquent, so there!" Then off she would head to the marketplace to catch the school bus.

Lost ground, though? Lost ground. She was fourteen. She was lanky and spotty and several inches taller than both Nelly and Myrtle, which meant she no longer received Myrtle's castoffs. Unlike other girls with available mothers or older sisters, she had no one around from whom she could borrow stockings, shoes, dresses, or skirts, no one with whom she could learn about makeup (or borrow it from them; Nelly only used rouge pale pink powder and a drop of "Evening in Paris" on special occasions).

Elner lived alone with an increasingly reclusive grandmother in a village (claiming to be a small town) two bus rides from anywhere. Her pocket money was less than that of others her age, as Stan spent his money on petrol for travelling from and back to London, treating his wife at the weekend and paying Nelly for Elner's keep. As a result, it now seemed to Elner as if she never went anywhere or met anyone except Nelly's friends.

Classmates had their own bedrooms with their own wardrobe, bookcase, and transistor radio or record player (or at least shared with a sibling, not a granny). They went on holidays. They went to towns and even visited bookshops, museums, and other places of historical or cultural interest. Parents took them to the theater to see the latest big pictures, to the swimming pool or the ice rink, a zoo or a stately home. They had something to talk about, reflect on. Their worlds were ever expanding both intellectually and socially. They were invited to mixed birthday parties of parents' friends' teenage boys. Elner had none of this. She had even given up two of the rare things that had previously given her pleasure. One of these was singing, although this proved temporary as she was able to work around Nelly's organizing here.

She had started going to St. Thomas' Church choir practice. Their organist and choirmistress was a good young musician, Beatrice Woodhall. She was friendly with Fred, who admired her and enjoyed chatting to her if she passed by while he stood at the corner, smoking his pipe and watching out for the pony-trekkers, who produced useful free manure for Fred's roses. So for a few months prior to Fred's death, Elner had slipped along to St. Thomas'—only for the practices—and had enjoyed Anglican choral singing. Uncle Ernie no longer led the Sunday school, and Rev. and Mrs. Collins had moved to a chapel in Gateshead. Elner had recently heard Anglican friends talking of confirmation classes. It sounded interesting…

After Fred's death, though, Mr. Ayre had been appointed organist at High Street Methodist Chapel. When he called at Nelly's house for the organ keys, Nelly asked him if his daughters would call for Elner on their way to Sunday school. This was extremely annoying! It meant that once again, Elner was unable to eat Sunday lunch with Nelly and Stan (and Annie, if not at work). But the reason behind this move was probably Nelly's manipulation of Stan. She wanted him to have Sunday lunch at Stanhope, not at Wearhead. However, Elner, as a third former at the new school, was able to join the school choir, really enjoyed the annual nine lessons and carols in Wolsingham Church.

However, the other even more important thing that Elner had lost was art. Initially, she had done so deliberately but had only intended to drop it for a year. After all, she had been top of 2A in art at the end of the second form with ninety-six percent. The trouble was that some timetabling idiot had put DS and art together, with German as an alternative (or woodwork and metalwork for boys).

Elner liked the thought of German but did not like domestic science, and the treadle sewing machines did not like her. She could never get the thread from the shuttle to come up under the needle. It just tangled instead. As for cooking, well, Nelly was a cook and didn't want competition but had that already to some extent from Annie. So better to drop DS completely and return to art in the fourth form. She intended to take art and German as two of her three optional subjects. Sadly, the third option had to be a science.

Such was Elner's plan, at the end of the third form. She explained it to Stan after the summer holidays. "I don't know anything about any of this," was his reply. "Go and ask the headmaster. He knows what he's doing."

Obediently, Elner talked to the head, who had his own timetabling concerns and was of the opinion that "little girls in the A stream ought to be doing Latin with German and aiming toward studying modern languages at university." But, she suggested, couldn't she take art with 4B, while 4A had singing? After all, she wouldn't be missing out on singing as she was in the school choir anyway. (She didn't add that class singing was really a waste of time, with the altos spending their time rolling aniseed balls under the piano to annoy Ida the spider, while the boys peeped out from the stage curtains and pulled faces at the girls. As the boys' voices were breaking or had just broken, they were allowed an extra private study period!)

"No," said the head. "Nine subjects were nine. Art would not be one of them. Go away and learn your Latin."

But a lot of it was rote learning, and Nelly, who left school the day she was thirteen, was not keen on checking anything for her or believed something foreign was wrong because Elner was pronouncing it correctly.

There was another subject too, which Elner was giving up. It never occurred to anyone that it would be useful to her, even though she had been third in it in the final term of 3A. This other subject was religious education. Dropping two of her best subjects caused her position in class to drop, but this also never occurred to anyone. She was deemed not to be trying as hard as she could on the conveyor-belt school system and, at the end of the fourth form, received a headmasterly comment in red ink: "Should do better."

(While Elner never did go on from her sixth form to study modern languages at a university, she did, at other points in her life, study art to bachelor's level and eventually gain a master's in theology and ministry. Yes, the languages would come in useful in real life too but were not where her heart lay at that time. She did O and A level without particular interest in anything that she was studying, except for English, cartography (as an art substitute) and one or two French romantic poets.

School had, once over, been a source of stability for Elner, a stability that home did not provide. She had always, before, enjoyed learning new things. Now, school let Elner down. It became grim, uninteresting, something to struggle through.

The local library also let her down. When she became fourteen, she was supposed to borrow books from the adult section, but the choice was limited and boring. Romances and Westerns were what most adult villagers fancied! Elner thus discovered the little-used shelves of science fiction and biography. (There was no English literature and precious little ancient history there either, after all.)

Instead of grumbling that Elner "lacks concentration at vital moments during the lesson," did it never occur to her teachers to offer encouragement rather than criticism? Strangely enough, in the long run, it was the Sunday school annoyance that proved useful to her. The Ayres and Sykses (or Airs and Graces, according to Stan) would call on a Sunday and take Elner to Sunday school with them. It was particularly galling to Elner that the eldest of these four girls was a year and a half younger than Elner. But Nelly approved of this arrangement, involving the children of two teachers on the one hand and a bank manager on the other. Nelly was Nelly, not to be done.

After Uncle Ernie had left the Sunday school, it muddled along until Marion Turner was announced as the new superintendent, with one or two new ideas. There was to be a junior youth club on Friday evenings from six to seven. It mainly involved "keep fit," as Mrs. Turner was a PE teacher. But as this was noncompetitive and nearly everyone else was younger than her, Elner coped, even becoming fitter! The Sunday school started entering the Youth Eisteddfod once again, becoming increasingly competitive, although Stanhope

Gilmore and Wolsingham Wesley generally topped the league tables back then.

Not long afterward, the cranky Methodist minister, who had replaced Mr. Collins and who had spent a lot of time in disagreement with Fred, left. He was replaced by a probationer minister, John Carr, who started up a senior youth club at the "rival" chapel Gilmore. There was music, table tennis, snooker, and a coffee bar—also, films or talks from time to time. The most memorable was probably by Jack Woodhall, who was not only the leader of Uncle Maurice's dance band but also the leader of the local volunteer fire brigade. He explained what to do if trapped in a fire while hopefully recruiting new volunteers from among the older lads.

At one point, there was going to be a play, but either it never happened or Elner was ill when it did. The plot behind getting the young folk to meet up together in a friendly manner was probably the threat of amalgamating the two chapels sooner or later.

Elner, however, remembered a particularly galling incident on her way home from High Street with the Airs and Graces. She had been drawing cartoons and inventing comic verses about school and youth club when one of the others, middiscussion, remarked, "You never talk about anything else but school." It occurred to Elner that she actually never *did* anything else, while these other girls were taken off to fun places by their parents on a frequent basis. Perhaps the girls' parents had more understanding of Elner's situation, though, including her in trips to Consett baths and once to the ballet.

Shortly after the youth club opened, J. F. Kennedy was assassinated. Elner and one or two others were standing by the table tennis table when Peter Bowes brought the news.

Both Sunday school and youth club gave Elner the chance to use her artistic talents once again, producing posters to go on display in the post office window right in the middle of the Front Street. Elner was pleased to see her work on display, especially on Thursday afternoons after school, when she collected Nelly's pension on her way home from the school bus.

Because of the long summer holidays of "nothing to do and nowhere to go," Elner volunteered for the trip to school camp between third and fourth form. The campsite was a farmer's field at Beadnell on the Northumberland coast. The weather was reasonably good, except for the day of the trip to the Farne Islands, when the campers were on the first boat out. Elner enjoyed that boat journey, and when one or two of the others felt seasick afterward, she was able to enjoy extra spam sandwiches.

This was a bygone age of letter writing, and Nelly had been deserted by both Elner and Stan at the same time, so wrote the following letter to the camp site.

I was pleased to have your letter this morning. I hope you are having a very nice time & that the weather is good for you all. Today is very wet here, but we've had a wonderful weekend.

You know, Eleanor, Uncle Maurice, Aunty Jessie, Judith and I were looking for you on Sunday night. We were right by your camp and stayed quite a while, but no sign of Eleanor. We had been to Holy Island. It would be about half past eight when we left your camp. Got home about half eleven. I've been all right, but missed you. Yesterday Uncle Maurice took Aunties Evelyn, Jessie and I for another run—went to Blanchland, Hexham and back by Allendale.

Aunty is here today so there's always someone around… I'm going up to Stanhope Hall tomorrow night. Don't forget to send Aunty a card.

Have a good time, pet. See you soon. Daddy and Annie got off all right on Sunday morning 7o/c then they phoned from the office in London just after we had dinner to say that they had a good journey down. Love, Nonna.

In spite of the attention and trips out, Nelly was obviously not happy by herself in the house. Stan and Annie were off on a trip to

Italy paid for by Aunty. Nelly must have been to Maurice and Jessie's for Sunday dinner because she was otherwise home alone.

For Elner, away in a tent on the Northumbrian coast, something of the beauty of seascape and unspoiled beaches, the wildlife, and the continuing historical presence of Aidan, Cuthbert, and Oswald in that place found its way into her heart. Next, though, came a big adventure because of the snowstorm at the start of '63.

By that time, Maurice had left Redmires and his Westgate home and taken a job as quarry manager of the Durhills Quarry, way out in the wilds of Collier Law on Stanhope Common. This job included a lovely luxury central-heated bungalow for the family and their cats. They moved in and enjoyed the peace.

Then came a winter's Saturday. Judith needed a trip to Bishop Auckland for clothes shopping, so Maurice drove her there, while Jessie and Maxwell stayed at home, watching TV. While Maurice and Judith were in Bishop, a chill wintry shower started, turning rapidly to sleet and snow on their homeward journey. At Stanhope, they turned off up Crawleyside, but by the time they got to the cattle grid, the road home was impassable, so they turned around and went to stay at Nelly's. Stan was also stuck there, unable to travel either to work in London or to Annie at Wearhead.

Meanwhile, up on the fell, the electricity stopped working, and food (especially for the cats) started running out. However, the phone still worked. After the storm abated and the council snowblower—the only one in England—started clearing the Crawleyside road, it was decided to mount an expedition up to Fellhaven (the bungalow's name) with provisions. Judith borrowed an old pair of Stan's trousers, necessary provisions were readied, and somehow a paraffin heater had been unearthed and packed onto Elner's old sledge. Expedition members to carry the goods were Maurice, Judith, Stan, and Elner.

The road was cleared to within a mile or two of the bungalow, where there was a useful space to leave Stan's car. They climbed out, unloaded everything, but didn't attempt to follow the road, knowing that it could be many feet under the snow in places. Instead, the plan was to follow what had once been a mineral line railway along the ridge, where the snow would be blasted downhill. There were telegraph poles marking this route.

It was a long, exhausting, but exhilarating journey, nevertheless, especially for Judith, whose borrowed trousers kept slipping. But eventually, they reached journey's end, the heater was lit, and whisky and cake were brought out to revive the explorers.

Of course, Stan and Elner still had to walk all the way back to the car, but they were relieved to see that the snowblower had appeared and was not far away. Most of the walk back would be along a cleared road! Elner still has photos showing herself dwarfed by ten-foot snowdrifts! That was one of several *big* Weardale storms.

Chapter 11

O-level year for Elner and biology was a nightmare. Fifty or more fifteen- and sixteen-year-olds—a mixture of A, B, and C—plunging into a lab and fighting over lab stools, fighting for the discomfort of a double lesson with no backrest.

"Watch carefully," says the teacher, holding up a small sheep's eye and a scalpel.

Elner looks fixedly out of the window instead.

After the mocks, it looks possible for Elner to pass eight out of nine subjects. Her English language looks very promising indeed, but at the other end of the scale, she only has twenty-five percent for biology. She writes a silly poem:

> "All I want for Christmas is 9 passes,
> Just like Rina Gray's or Brian Cass's"

Meanwhile, Stan has just learned that he will soon be made redundant. Motorways are the coming thing; railways are falling out of fashion. In time, he will go back to working for Redmires in Wolsingham. Meanwhile, things are transitional.

Back, then, to Elner's school, where a holiday to Switzerland is proposed. Only, two years previously, the fully employed Stan had taken the fully employed Annie off on holiday to Italy (Italy, of all places—Elner's part heritage), and Aunty had footed the bill for Stan, her son substitute, and his local Weardale wife, disapproved of by Nelly and Fred. Elner really wants to go on this trip—it would be her first time abroad. All her Stanhope youth club friends are going. So?

"You can go if you pay for yourself!" was the adults' ultimatum. And so she did, using over a decade's worth of school Monday morning savings money, plus all the other funds deposited in her Post Office Savings account all the way back to that half crown from the *Auckland Chronicle* coloring competition. Once, when she was nine or ten, her savings had been her "horse fund," but now she was not going to be left behind by those friends who reckoned she had nothing to talk about but school!

During exam periods, it was possible for pupils to arrive at school or go home by means of service buses rather than hanging about in school, cluttering up the dining room or library. One early afternoon, Elner's exam had finished, and she arrived home, only to find the back door wide open and Nelly nowhere to be seen. Elner heads off down the garden and searches diligently in case Nelly has had a fall and is lying hurt down there at the bottom of the steps. No Nelly. Elner worries, and the worries push revision from her mind.

Over the past two and a half years since Fred's death, the balance has been changing gradually. Who exactly is the carer of whom these days? Which of them is the more responsible? In this instance, it turns out that either Maurice or Humphrey has taken Nelly for a ride. Well, a note would have been helpful, although Nelly refuses to write notes! It would have been useful if, whichever erring uncle it was, had had enough common sense to check that Nelly had at least closed the back door. But Nelly has always been their authority figure.

Finally, the exams were over, and Elner was about to take part in sports day for the first time ever. She had accidentally discovered, having stopped growing and adjusted to her asymmetrical self, that she is reasonably capable of running. It was an accidental discovery. Mrs. Mac, the PE teacher, was doing the standards with the grammar stream girls, and Elner was to run 220 yards with a couple of girls from another form. *Oh*, she thought, looking at them, *I can probably keep up with them.* And so she did, not knowing that the smaller of the two had been in the county sports regularly.

Thus, she accidentally surprised herself with a two-point standard (fast time!) and took part in the sports over the last three years of school. In her final year, she was in the winning four-by-one-hundred-yard relay, when they set a new record (although admittedly, the other three girls went on to become PE teachers). She also managed to be third in the 440 yards.

At the end of term, Elner and her Stanhope friends looked forward to the holiday. Peter Bowes, geography teacher, was the organizer. There were two sets of two separate buses, and students were to be divided according to year groups. Upper sixth and fifth forms on the A buses, lower sixth and fourth forms on B buses. But that meant that Elner (fifth form) would be on a different bus from Rina and Elizabeth (lower sixth) and "Grace" and Anne (fourth form). Instead, she was stuck with classmates with whom she had little in common!

The problem was even greater because the route was circular. The A buses would travel clockwise while the B buses went anticlockwise once they crossed the channel. Thus, her friends would be visiting Brussels, Luxemburg, Nancy, and Epinal, while Elner went via Rheims and Besancon. They would not meet up again until the hotel in Switzerland; but even then, they would be eating their meals half an hour apart! And even shared rooms (three or four pupils to each) and visits to places of interest had been allocated on the basis of "same forms." Thus, Elner, having had to pay for her holiday with her life savings rather than being parentally subsidized as others were, then had to spent most of her holiday parted from the very friends she thought she was going to be with! She was very annoyed with Peter Bowes.

The separate tours were to Lucerne (where she bought a Switzerland hat), Berne (where she bought a tiny wooden bear), "Lauterbrunnen and Grindelwald," and "Kandersteg and the Blue Lake." At least, though, she could spend the free time half days with her friends in Interlaken or just on a country walk, admiring the mountains, the Heidi-ish rural landscapes, and the foreign variation on haymaking.

The visit to the glacier did not go smoothly, however. They arrived at the bottom of a rock face. Rickety wooden steps, around five hundred or so, wound vertiginously upward. Elner sought out Peter Bowes. "Sir, I can't go up there."

"Oh, yes, you can! Go on! Off you go. Don't be silly."

Give Elner her due; she psyched herself into completing three fifths of the climb before totally freezing, then her legs could carry her no further. Miss Defty took pity on her, sat her on a rock safely away from the edge, and gave her a drink of lemonade to revive her. It took a crocodile of teachers (two ahead and one behind, but none of whom was the offending Peter Bowes) to get her safely back down. As for the glacier, she would just have to imagine it or buy a postcard.

The return trip to England was less interesting. Luxemburg seemed very modern. There was a funfair in Brussels and chips for sale, very like England. They crossed the channel and headed north for the GCE results. Marking was very different back then. Only the top five percent of candidates in the country gained a grade 1, regardless of whether others were worthy of such a mark. The next ten percent gained a 2, the next ten percent a 3, and so on.

Looked at in that light, Elner was in the top fifteen percent in the country for English literature; the top twenty-five percent for English language, French, geography, history; the top thirty-five percent for maths; and the top fifty-five percent for biology. But she slipped into somewhere just below that fifty-five percent in Latin and German—let down, in fact, by the headmaster's options for her. She only had seven passes, not nine. She was a failure because only those with eight or nine passes were awarded on speech day. At Christmas, she passed her resit German, and in the summer, she passed the Latin, although not enjoying the set books nearly so well (the rest of the country must have been poor). If only she had been allowed to take art!

The new term started, and being in possession of more than five O levels, she became a sixth former with a new badge for her blazer: *prudens qui perficit* indeed! Her youth club friend Rina Gray was suddenly transformed into the head girl, and she herself had a decision to make—choosing three subjects from those in which she had gained her best marks. Now if only history had been her idea of real history (social and cultural history in far-off times), she would have been truly interested, but European politics in the last century was not interesting to her at all.

Thus, she opted for English literature, French, and geography. At least with geography, there was some drawing (aka cartography and projected profiles) and human beings in general, with different cultures and responses to climate, currents, and physical geography. The down side of her choice of geography was that Peter Bowes was her teacher.

In the lower sixth too, everyone took the Use of English exam necessary for entrance to some universities. There were interesting add-ons to the curriculum for one term only too because the school was about to undergo a general inspection. Thus, something entitled "Minority Time" had been invented and was about to prove interesting.

But before Elner arrived at Minority Time, while she was still only a week into the sixth form, another unsettling event occurred (most annoyingly over Stanhope Show weekend), causing longer-term family rifts for Nelly to play with and expand on. Fernanda suddenly announced that she was paying her long-lost daughter a visit! She and Mario, her second husband, were on holiday in London and intended to make the journey to the North East for a couple of nights so that Fernanda could see Elner again.

Stan decided that Fernanda and her husband, Mario, should stay at Stanhope Hall and duly made arrangements. His cousin Harry and wife Alma had started up a kind of preagritourism business in the central part of the Norman Hall building (complete with ghost, if Alma was to be believed).

Meanwhile, however, Maurice and Jessie, who had kept up communications with Fernanda, felt that she and Mario should stay up on the fell with them. Determined in their plan, they drove to the station, collected the visitors, and took them to Fell Haven. This angered Stan, who felt that his brother had no right to interfere in matters that were his sole business. Nelly stirred both of them up as that added spice to life. What with that and some fuss over Maxwell's wedding, the two brothers ended up not speaking to each other for several months!

Fernanda arrived at, or at least passed through, Stanhope while Elner and pals were in St. Thomas' (Norman) Church, for the annual ecumenical show service, which the fairground people also attended, before heading off to their winter quarters. Meanwhile, Fernanda and Mario were being whisked off to Fell Haven. For Elner, that day, there was no Sunday school because of the band concert (Elner was by now a Sunday school teacher). Then came the dash from the Castlefield to the Rodham Monument at Newtown for the farewell piece by the visiting band (always by a prize-winning brass band Black Dyke, Fairy Aviation, or one of the others).

> Sunset, by the Rodham Monument
> Today we had no sun
> and now, at last, "fast falls the eventide"
> "Abide with me" (a solo trumpeter)
> Old folk remember shows and friends gone by.
> Old soldiers bring to mind their DLI.
> For home is Stanhope, after all, for those who stand around.
> Drizzle drenches faces that are grateful for the rain.

Then came the after-chapel young-folks get-together (with food) at the Manse. And next morning, of course, there was school. But when she got home, laden with homework, there was her mother and Mario. Elner generally had her tea at that time before settling down to do her homework.

But first, this teatime, there were photos to be taken. The first of these (in black-and-white) showed a group of four females—from left to right: Nelly, Elner, Fernanda, and Annie. All are smiling, Nelly and Elner looking directly into the camera, Fernanda looking sideways at Elner, and Annie somewhat dazzled by the sun. Elner is the tallest member of this group. Her mother is slightly taller than Annie. Nelly is about the same height as Elner's ear. Nelly is wearing a short-sleeved blouse and a light-colored skirt.

Despite her smile, her eyes are wary and worried. Annie sports a sleeveless dress and high heels. Fernanda is in a blouse, skirt, and modestly heeled shoes. She also wears a cardigan, and her arms are folded. Elner is in school uniform—white shirt blouse, blue tie with red and yellow stripes, scarlet cardigan, white ankle socks, and flat black shoes. For some inexplicable reason lost to memory, both forefingers point footward. Is this some sign of adolescent rebellion perhaps? She repeats the same gesture in the photo of just her and Fernanda, where Fernanda has a cigarette in her left hand.

On a third photo, Elner and Fernanda have changed ends. Elner is now wearing even more clothing (the school blazer with its new sixth-form badge and house badge [Dale]). Fernanda, on the other hand, has stripped off the protective cardigan so that her smart spotted silk armless blouse is visible. She is clutching Elner's right arm, so the fingers and feet gesture is not repeated here.

After this photo session, everyone went back indoors. The adults were planning a meal out over the fells at the Lord Crewe Arms (posh). Maurice and Jessie would be there too, but Elner is not invited—never has been invited to places where adults eat out, except on the previous October's visit to London, where Stan took her to a steak house once to eat. Regarding social niceties, they tended to keep her retarded as that worked out less expensive. This evening, she has homework to be completed before the next day. First, though, she will be fed. Oh, dear!

Nelly proudly places a plate in front of her while everyone watches. A small tin's worth of Heinz spaghetti on toast. "Look," exclaims Nelly, "I even feed her Italian food!"

Not only does everyone watch her eat, Fernanda takes to stroking her proprietorially while she strives to consume her repast. Finally, Mario suggests that perhaps Fernanda should desist, allowing Elner to eat in peace.

After tea, Elner heads upstairs with the excuse of French homework. She takes her satchel into Stan and Annie's occasional bedroom, having to pretend that this warm, sunny bedroom is hers. Fernanda, former university student of foreign languages, pursues her, offering homework help. Elner produces her French literature homework. Fernanda peruses textbooks and questions and decides to leave her to it, after all.

Back to school, then, with the emphasis as usual being on what she had *not* achieved, never on what she had. It was as if her schoolmates were from a different planet—that of normality. Elner, on the other hand, was coming to the conclusion that she was like a slot machine. Her adults put next to nothing in but grumbled about the lack of jackpot. Obviously, she wasn't trying. Her teachers sang a similar tune too:

> I would be happier if she showed more enthusiasm and desire to enter class discussions.

> Wide reading will give confidence during class discussions.

> Elner seems to lack concentration at vital moments during lessons.

> She has ability in oral work and literature, though the language work has too many errors.

> Most commendable (result). If she can overcome her lack of confidence she should do well.

People who are good at class discussions tend to be those who come from a home where discussion takes place. Poor Elner did try to engage Nelly and Aunty in discussions, but the answer was generally, "Stop arguing the point," "Why do you ask the road you know?" or (more harshly) "Why do you want to know the far end of a fart and where the stink blows to?"

Her friends were in different year groups, taking different subjects, and more likely wanting to talk about such gossip as who was going with whom at that time.

Wide reading? Oh, ho, what exactly could she read? Now, Rina Gray was taking science subjects—botany, zoology, and chemistry. Her mother was an incredible person. She had worked as a hairdresser before marriage, but as Rina grew, so Mrs. Gray also nurtured ever widening interests. They went to *bookshops* and found enjoyable things in them. They bought books! They discussed the contents of their books with each other and with P. C. Gray. They were mentally alert, not stagnant. Until Elner was almost nineteen and living in a place where bookshops were accessible, she had no means of travel to faraway bookshops.

The Ayre girls, whose father taught French, arranged for his daughters to spend several weeks, two summers running, *avec* a French family on the French coast, speaking nothing but French. Obviously, this improved their chances in both oral and grammatical French.

And, generally speaking, Elner's fellow students had parents who cared enough about their children's education to discuss with them what would be helpful and how they were finding their sixth-form life, basically just encouraging their kids and caring as best they could. Whereas Nelly, like Elner, was "failing" and Stan pursuing an unsettled road from Somersons (in London) to Redmires (in Wolsingham) to Fillcrete (throughout the whole Northern England and Scotland area) during this time. He certainly had no time to waste on shopping trips to bookshops. Any time he had to waste was spent in the Cowshill Hotel with Annie. (Oh, use your brains, teachers!)

Finally, when Elner reached the upper sixth, Mrs. Bainbridge, who probably knew more of her family difficulties than the other teachers, finally did so.

But, back to the lower sixth and Minority Time. This was theorized as expanding the interests of sixth-form pupils at a time when they were increasingly concentrated on three A levels. Three Minority Time options were thus provided to render the sixth formers more "civilized." Students had to choose two of the three.

Elner chose art history and ethics, the third option being science based. Ethics was led by the RE teacher and, of course, involved discussion of topical issues, and while Elner did not participate in the discussions, that did not mean that she was not formulating ideas. She was, just as she was in the classroom when teachers believed she "lacked concentration." But her favorite Minority Time was, of course, art history, with slides of the works being an encouragement and revelation to her. Oh, very gradually, this was the shape of things to come.

Chapter 12

Elner wrote this poem a few years later, and it was published in a small-press poetry magazine called *Here Now* back in the early '70s. She was probably thinking back to Nelly at that time.

"Old Woman in a Mirror"

So old—your hands a map of veins.
Your feet unbalance you.
So cold—returning to the house alone
that once housed two.
You knew that age would come and yet
haytimes and new years passed
to your last act.
Now nearly all is told—
except, your meaning stays illusive, and
how shrunk that person is who seemed so grand.

Elner, the sixth-form version, had different priorities from her classmates. They were the teens of the Swinging Sixties in the age of the Beatles and the Rolling Stones. For them, life energies were focused outward, directed toward others around them—all that girl-friend and boyfriend stuff.

Having witnessed a divorce being enacted before her very eyes between the ages of four and seven, and at times having to act out a part in it, Elner was disinclined to believe the Cinderella myth of the gullible. She despaired of the scenes being enacted in front of her. Her classmates were thoughtlessly using other people as status symbols, as things rather than people, to prove their own positions in an arbitrary pecking order of desirability.

Elner cultivated an outer raiment of caution, the one that her teachers misread as withdrawal from participation. At school and youth club, she felt more like an undercover agent in a foreign country with strange customs. She preferred the satire of TW3 and the lyrics of Paul Simon to the pop revolution "circus" as well. In the ethos of her times, she was weird!

Well, all right, she'd had crushes on one or two males in the past: a young teacher, an older boy who used to try and steal her school beret as she was about to get off the bus. (After all, this latter was at least providing "attention" or acknowledgement of her existence.) But she preferred to keep her fancies unobtainable. Besides, the louder and more self-important boys in the geography group's prime interest was in underage drinking to prove how adult they were! One of the underage drinkers was also the only boy taking French. In fact, he was the only other person taking the same choices as Elner. But at least in English, a couple of the other boys—Geoff from the youth club gang and Ben—were more "civilized."

Perhaps the underage drinkers struck her as stupid because of her father's affection for pubs, which would grow into an addiction a few years later. His three main loves were Annie, the pub, and his mother's favor—while, like Topsy, Elner felt she had "just grow'd" as an afterthought in people's lives. In short, she was a moody teenager deprived of outlets or interests in which she could express herself. Trying to explain anything to Nelly was to be accused of "twining" (grumbling), a crime that Nelly had accused her of ever since she started school.

However, Elner's first priority was mere survival, not just her own survival but most especially the survival of Nelly. Should Nelly die within Elner's sixth-form time, who knew what would happen. She would possibly be homeless, or Annie would expect Stan to put her out to work instead of being a "kept" seventeen-to-eighteen-year-old.

Elner was often told about Annie's wonderful cousin Brenda in much the same way that Nelly extolled marvelous Myrtle. Now, both Brenda and Myrtle were very nice girls, but the adoration of them made them much less interesting as friend material. Brenda had been in the same form as Elner since 2A, and sometimes a shared sense of mischief had united them. They had both been in the same (winning) group on the camping holiday at Beadnell too. But Brenda was always in the top three or four in the class, a main cause for Annie's boasting. The school was pushing Brenda to apply for Oxford, along with another girl, Kathy Oates.

Brenda's dad was a miner, and she lived near Crook. That meant she was only one bus away from both Bishop Auckland and Durham. Durham had student bookshops. Bishop Auckland had part-time Saturday jobs. Brenda had gained for herself a Saturday job in a shoe shop, with staff discount on footwear, and Annie wondered why Elner couldn't do likewise. Elner pointed out the differences in location, cost of transport (more than her pocket money—hint), and an hour or more extra time spent on bus travel, but all to no avail. In addition (but not to be mentioned or explained), Elner's "day off" from carer duties was a Sunday—the day after Stan and Annie had stayed overnight at Nelly's—thus depriving Elner of ever having a room of her own. So Elner did her homework on a Saturday. Every Saturday, there was a nonsense geography essay to be written—by "nonsense," I mean topics outside of the curriculum (landlocked states, dairy farming in Australia, etc.).

Brenda didn't take geography, so her weekend homework burden was somewhat different from Elner's. It was also quite possible that her parents showed an interest in her existence and an appreciation of her efforts, encouraging her and being proud of her. They were even prouder when, in the UVIMS, Brenda succeeded Rina Gray as head girl. Elner's lot, meanwhile, just expected jackpot without investments such as encouragement.

During the Easter holidays of Elner's lower sixth year, Mr. Carr, the Methodist minister, had arranged for a student mission from Cliff College to visit the Stanhope Chapels. There was sunshine corner every morning, a picnic up on the fells, a football game on the castle field, and a sponsored walk to Wearhead Chapel for charity.

There were various extra services too, including one at Rookhope. At the end of the sermon at Rookhope, there was a call to all who wanted to give their lives to Jesus to go to the front, and a fair number of the young folk, including Elner's friends, went forward. Elner did not. Analyzing this, Elner reckoned that they were more subject to emotional manipulation than she was. Either that or her heavenly Parent, just like the earthly ones, didn't particularly want her. On the last Sunday, though, at High Street, Elner, angry for God's not wanting her either, decided she would go forward anyway, whether God liked it or not! But she remained forever unconvinced about the efficacy of this type of evangelism.

She had worked out a theory of the Trinity being the divine equivalent of body (Jesus), mind (God the Father), and spirit (Holy Spirit). As a human, she had body, mind, and soul and needed to give exercise to each part. So when what had been Tinkler's fields became redesigned as a set for building Bondisle Way, she was able to slip down the garden and run a circuit of cinder track to prepare herself for the 440 yards, training herself to have energy for a sprint finish.

Romance was in the air during that visit. Everyone seemed to be pairing off. Three Cliff College students started friendships—Rina with Winston, a Jamaican singer; Jean (one of the future PE teachers) with a tall blond and handsome lad from the south; and Katy, a year or two older and working, with Trevor. Meanwhile, among the locals, two Gilmore boys, Geoff and Billy, started going with Grace and Anne from High Street. Another Gilmore boy, Frank, had begun a friendship with Elizabeth from Westgate that would last a lifetime. Basically, in Elner's opinion, they were all mad, and she was more alone than ever.

After walking to Wearhead Chapel via Slit Wood with the others, she opted to start walking back on her own and was east of Eastgate before being picked up. Increasingly, she was finding more comfort in her own company. Even as a prefect, she worked alone, although this was Mrs. Bainbridge's idea of helping her toward wider reading. Elner was appointed library prefect. Mostly, this consisted of chasing courting couples out of the library and ensuring that they hadn't messed up the Dewey Decimal System. But when new stock arrived, she had the dinnertime task of cataloguing the clean, pristine volumes fresh from their packaging. From time to time, she would find something relevant to a homework essay and asked permission from "Mrs. B." to borrow it for the weekend.

The English set books that she found most interesting were *King Lear* and *Sons and Lovers*. In French, she preferred the Romanic poets, especially Victor Hugo. She was living out the "youth and age" conflicts of *King Lear* in her everyday life and had her own theory about how the play should be cast—specifically, that the woman playing Cordelia should also play the Fool. It was Lear's line, on learning of Cordelia's death: "And my poor Fool is dead," that gave her the idea. Cordelia, having married the French king, would have had to use a disguise; otherwise, she would be killed as a traitor. But there she is "out i' the night, i' the storm," suffering the disquietude of a dethroned king who made a foolish choice. Elner also saw something of Nelly in the possessiveness of Mrs. Morell for her sons, with Nelly sometimes pitting Maurice and Stan against each other. And like the grandmother in Hugo's *Souvenir de la Nuit du Quattrieme*, Nelly is mourning the loss of all she once held dear. None of it was any longer hers.

Sometimes, then, when Elner seemed to lack concentration at vital moments during the lesson, she was merely constructing relevance between the set books and her home situation. At other times, though, the events outside the glass wall-of-windows were simply more relevant than the set books. It was summertime. Outside, a lower form in PE kit were scattered about the grounds doing discus, javelin, shot put, running, long jump, or high jump. One boy was very determined to perfect the new (then) way of doing the high jump—backward and headfirst. It was an odd movement and would be more difficult to draw than ever the long jump painting she had done in 2A had been. That painting had been on show for several open nights, occasions that Elner always missed as she was never able to produce a parent or guardian to be her plus one!

Intrigued, she watched the boy's progress but was distracted by something in the classroom. When she looked outside again, the boy was lying motionless in the sandpit at the other side of the jump. Someone brought the male PE teacher over. A crowd of classmates collected and were dispersed to the changing rooms, making way for ambulance and doctor. The boy had broken his neck and did not survive.

The previous summer term, the Stanhope school bus had been involved in a crash with a laden wagon. Elner had been one of a handful of Stanhope pupils on the Rookhope bus that year. It had been ahead of the Stanhope one, and Elner remembered afterward a loud noise behind them, just before they reached Frosterley. In that crash, two younger girls, still at the old school, were killed.

Two years running, then, the school had suffered tragedies. Tragedy struck again in Elner's upper sixth year. One Friday afternoon, one of the now-of-age drinker boys, a boy Peter Bowes had entered for S-level geography as well as A level—one of the good students but the only one who took exactly the same subjects as Elner—was not feeling very well. He had a sore throat, a headache, and seemed to be starting with flu. Peter advised him to go home and have an early night, but the boy Philip replied that his older brother was home from the merchant navy, and they had planned a night out at Bishop. So in spite of his illness, Philip went out with his brother but never returned.

While the two lads were heading home from the night out, the car skidded off the road at Harperley Banks and hit a tree. Doors buckled open, and in this age before seat belts, Philip's brother was tossed onto the grassy verge, while Philip, who was driving, landed on the road, unconscious but alive. But at that point, a car came flying down the hill behind them, ran over Philip, and disappeared into the darkness. This hit-and-run driver was never found.

So once again, for the third year running, tragedy struck the school. Elner was as sad as all the rest. For the past six years, Philip had been in most of the classes that she had attended. Philip's father was a near neighbor of Aunty and knew Nelly too. It was only natural that they expected her to join the large school group attending the funeral. She was on the staircase one day, just before the funeral, when the small lad who always sat next to Philip in geography stopped her. "Why are *you* going to the funeral? He *hated* you."

Elner could not understand this. She had never bothered either of these boys. Perhaps it was that they believed Peter Bowes was marvelous while she didn't for several reasons: because he picked on her in class and "made game" of her; because he seemed to have done his best to mess up her first trip abroad; and, going back to first and second form, Peter had given her good marks while courting her cousin

Judith but had dropped the marks when they broke up. Despite being in the geography group of such a popular teacher, Elner was not a Peter Bowes fan, unlike those sycophant boys or Barbara and Janis.

She went to the funeral anyway. Her adults expected it of her, and she was an adult too. A week or two later, Peter, being left with an S-level entry, which was now studentless, asked Elner if she wanted to take S level. She declined. (The following year, when Elner's classmates had dispersed all over the country, although nothing untoward happened to the current crop of students at Wolsingham, Annie's cousin Brenda was killed while hitchhiking from Leeds to London with a friend. But that was still to come beyond this narrative.)

The A levels were fast approaching, and the upper sixth had been sent away to revise at home, but Nelly was ill, so Nelly and Elner's territory was suddenly besieged by daytime aunts, occasional doctors, and Maurice and Stan after work. They all chattered and cluttered. Someone had taken to using a pneumatic drill in Dales Street as well just to add to the din. And there was Bondisle Way being built at the bottom of the garden.

Meanwhile, what had been the lawn and drying area for washing was being claimed by an ugly extension to the lodge dining room so that they could hire it out for functions. The only way to get any peace was to get up at six to grab a couple of hours of quiet revision.

One early evening, the living room being a chattery, Elner was lying on her stomach on the old proggy mat in the kitchen, chin on elbows and geography file open in front of her, when she caught the voice of Uncle Maurice, telling her dad, who'd just arrived, "So they're sending Mam for tests. Dr. Thomson thinks it might be cancer. But we mustn't tell Elner while she's doing her exams."

Elner, of course, having heard the secret conversation, picked up her file and walked off through the living room, to transhumant studies elsewhere so that they wouldn't find out that she'd heard.

One by one, the exams came and went to the scent of cut grass and the wailing of lawn mowing outside the windowless gym. In every gym exam down the years, Mr. Dand, the head, had always arrived to check in with the invigilators about five minutes or so before exam's end. You could set a clock by him, except…

Elner was busy with her French literature paper—one and a half questions to go and three quarters of an hour to write them in—when Mr. Dand walked into the gym. Elner stopped writing in anticipation while he talked to one of the invigilating teachers. There was an earlier bus; she knew that. He must have had a phone call and needed to tell her if she finished early and went off to catch the earlier bus. He would have to let her know, just in case, that Nonna had died. But panic set in, and writing wouldn't come. Was he going to take her out of the exam to tell her or just—no, he was about to sit down—wait until she finished. But the worrying undid the timing, and the last answer was a mess—what there was of it. And Nelly hadn't died, after all. Mr. Dand, for whatever unknown reason, had decided to invigilate for three quarters of an hour, causing Elner to mess up her French literature paper. The very person who had caused her to study languages in the first place.

After the exams, the upper sixth were expected to return to school on one particular day. Some of the boys headed off to the pub at lunch time and were duly removed from the prefect list. The girls instead went in for practical jokes. Elner was involved, along with Annie's cousin Brenda and Kathleen Wearmouth. Brenda, being agile, was able to lock half the lavatory doors from the inside and climb over (or squeeze under) the partition to the next one.

Elner and Kathleen were involved in an interesting trick whereby all the classes would be told individually (by their former wet-day prefect) that they had to be in the hall before 2:00 p.m. for a special assembly. Then, when the teacher for that class went to their usual classroom, there would be no class! Utter harmless confusion combined with good exercise, except that Elner was wet-day prefect for 3A and B girls, who were nice, well-behaved kids, who appreciated Elner's politeness toward them.

Unfortunately, some of them were due to have a lesson with Mrs. Bainbridge at two. She arrived early and knew that no school assembly meeting was scheduled for that time, so she sent for Elner and threatened to take away her prefect status. But the rest of the girl prefects involved in the practical joke supported her, and she realized that she couldn't sack all the girl prefects, and especially not the head girl, after half the boys were already sacked! They were told to save such tricks for university rag weeks instead!

Meanwhile, Nelly's test results had returned. The good news was that she did not have cancer; the bad news was that her aorta was dilating. She was weak but dressed each morning and engaged in light activities. She could not manage the bread making as the kneading was heavy work, and she refused to eat Baker Thompson's "shop" bread, so Elner, under Nelly's supervision, took on the role of bread maker!

She also did whatever food shopping had to be done. In the afternoons, while Nelly had her afternoon nap, as always, Elner was free to go on walks with whichever friends were around and available. Most often, this was Rina Gray, who was doing a summer zoology project on caddisfly larvae.

"A Life in the Day of a Caddis Fly Larva"
By Elner

The pond-safe caddis in its self-made shell,
(A thread-bound twig-or-pebble crust)
Secures itself around a nine-inch depth
Awaiting Protozoa, weed or grub
Until, one day, a special honour comes.
It leaves its stone for flask, or jar.
Its slime-world gone, a test-tube life begins,
Beyond the pond, in saucer's stagnant calm.
Misfortune then befalls all caddis life
When they are pushed from twig-fast coat.
The more adaptable use what they find
To build new homes, while others merely float.
The ones who build new coats from tail to head
Are then preserved to everlasting. Dead.

Elner produced useful bits of geographical thought to aid the scientific mind, intent on studying "beasties," such as:

> I can't understand. Both sets of caddis are from ponds in the same quarry, but the results are entirely different!
>
> Well, that pond is at the base of the quarry face, so may contain debris from the stone. It also has sun shining on it all day long, in good weather, so the water temperature will be different and the caddis' adaption to light. That other pond is on soil, a long way from the quarry face. It is mainly in shadow and has more vegetation growing around it. All those factors could cause variations.

Surprise, surprise! Elner gained a B in geography, but her other two (better) subjects were more or less dead in the water. Her proposed universities needed a B and two Cs, but no one at all in the A group gained a higher grade than E, while the B group (different teacher) gained higher marks. Her French, thanks to Mr. Dand's spot of invigilation, put her in the Laodicean "pass at O level" category. It meant neither pass nor fail. She had done sufficient to pass, so F would have been unjust. But this had been a good year for French, so the fifty-five percent of students with the lowest pass grades were awarded "pass at O level" (after two years' hard work and a pass grade).

No university wanted her, but she could not remain at home and do resits. Nelly was becoming weaker. Soon, Elner would no longer have a real home, merely a place of tolerance. With a sense of the usual failure, she packed her secondhand trunk and left for a teacher-training college nearly three hundred miles away.

Conclusion

After Elner left, Stan and Annie moved into Nelly's house full-time. An excerpt from a letter—Stan to Elner. No, there was no Facebook, Skype, or e-mail back then. People used long-distance phone calls once a week. Otherwise, everyone just used to write letters.

> Got Dr. Liddell to see Nonna this morning— gave her some capsules to take and I got her some "Complan" at the Dr's request—see if we can get her strength up a little. Dr. says her heart is "very, very bad." Well pet she has just got up and it seems she is looking for a run in the sunshine. (Aunty also). I am not sure yet about coming to Oxford next weekend.

Nelly, still "the boss," was, though.

> Daddy has just finished writing to you and asks me to put a line in. I just managed to get up 3.30 & he is going to take me for a little run out as the sun is shining and it may make me feel better. Looking forward to seeing you next weekend. Love, Nonna.

Nelly travelled to Lady Spencer-Churchill College two days later. She marveled at the recently opened college with its modern buildings and air of respectability. "Elner will do well here," she said. Elner sighed to herself. Nelly didn't understand the difference between a teacher training college and a university.

At half term, Elner took a train to the far north, along with one or two of the other N. E. college "refugees" from Durham or Newcastle. They had to stand all the way from Oxford to Birmingham. Reading another passenger's paper during this part of her journey was how Elner first learned of the Aberfan disaster, where 116 children and twenty-eight adults were killed in a colliery landslide. She had to change stations at Birmingham back in those days, racing across Central Brom with cases. Elner felt that the London underground from Paddington to King's Cross would have been easier and decided to return that way instead.

This was Nelly's final week of life. She was too weak to get up now, but she insisted on repeating to Elner what object should go to which relative when she died. She would not make a will; she just expected Elner to "see to things" and talked of family visitors as being like vultures gathering. She claimed she didn't want flowers at the funeral. People hadn't given her flowers while she was alive, so why bother now? But she had managed to persuade Stan to get Elner a nineteenth birthday present—a guitar. There were guitar lessons at college so that students could do singing with their school classes on teaching practice.

On the Sunday morning (Halloween), Elner said her last good-byes to Nelly before Stan drove her to Darlington Station, which in those days prided itself on owning Stephenson's Rocket and Locomotion Number 1 on the platform. Stan informed her that when Nelly died, she was *not* to return for the funeral.

She had a long, miserable wait at Paddington with the words of Paul Simon's "Homeward Bound" in her head: "I'm waiting at the railroad station, got a ticket for my destination…my suitcase and guitar in hand." She too wished to be homeward bound but had no home to go to, knowing that Nelly was dying.

Nelly died through the night, but the college never informed her until Monday's lectures were over. She was advised to go home for the funeral but replied that she had been ordered not to.

Stan and Annie got a brand-new council house in Bondisle Way. Most of Elner's childhood memorabilia were binned, and neither of the vases that Nelly said she should have been given actually came to her.

Elner's *How Not to Raise a Child* childhood was gone with Nelly. A few years later, she had an unexpected call to preach. *God can't mean me*, she thought, *Unless the Old Testament lesson says something suggesting I should.* Oh, dear! The lesson was from Isaiah 6!

But for now, we leave her feeling very alone at Lady Spencer-Churchill College–Oxford, where she was about to train to help other children achieve a better bargain or to help them through their own experiences of *How Not to Raise a Child*.

Lightning Source UK Ltd.
Milton Keynes UK
UKHW021454040522
402467UK00003B/18

9 781098 038373